A PASSIONATE PEOPLE

A Passionate People

*The personal stories of 17 leading
figures in the renewal of the church*

Wallace Boulton

eagle

Guildford, Surrey

British Library Cataloguing in Publication Data. A catalogue record for this book is available from the British Library.

Published by Eagle, an imprint of Inter Publishing Service (IPS) Ltd, PO Box 530, Guildford, Surrey GU2 5FH.

Typeset by Eagle
Printed by Cox & Wyman, Reading
ISBN No: 0 86347 322 9

Acknowledgements

My thanks are due to all those who readily agreed to meet me and talk about their life; to David Wavre at Eagle for inviting me to undertake this book and for his encouragement throughout; to Tony Collins at Monarch for his consent for me to make further use of those interviews which had appeared in *Renewal*; to Lis Millard, who transcribed most of the interviews, and last but not least, to my wife Marian for her understanding and support, as always.

CONTENTS

INTRODUCTION

'Forget the former things; do not dwell in the past. See, I am doing a new thing! Now it springs up; do you not perceive it?' (Isaiah 43:19, NIV). These words were addressed to Israel at a time of affliction. They are a reminder of God's promises and his faithfulness. Here too is surely a timely message for today's church. We read and hear so much about the church being in decline. Yet there is another side to the picture. God is indeed doing 'a new thing' in this generation. This is not an over-optimistic view. The Holy Spirit is bringing new life to the church. There is a resurgence at the roots. We are not seeing full-scale revival – not yet – but we have been seeing a renewal movement which is affecting growing numbers of people.

Consider, for instance, Alpha, a 15-session practical introduction to the Christian faith, which has grown from only five courses in 1992 to courses in 6,488 churches this year, plus over 4,000 overseas. With its simple formula of 'friends bringing friends', it has an approach which is attractive to non-churchgoers. It has spread from Holy Trinity Brompton and is proving effective in all kinds of places, from inner cities to rural areas. It has spread, too, across the denominations and streams, from the Pentecostals to Roman Catholics. More than 680,000 people have experienced Alpha courses in the UK and the worldwide figure has reached one million. The lives of many participants have been changed.

These courses are now running also in prisons, where chaplains are reporting with astonishment that prisoners who start the course as atheists are giving their lives to Christ at the end; they report too that there is an extraordinary impact on the lives of families and friends and that prison officers are becoming increasingly involved. Alpha has also been adapted to run in youth groups, the police force, the army, government offices, businesses and homelessness projects.

Consider too the new church movement, known originally as the house church movement. It developed from meetings in a few people's homes. Now, some 20 years on from the start of its networks, it has more than 120,000 members in this country. In many areas its congregations are among the largest. The new churches have become more willing to share in activities with other churches and have become more accepted by them. Many of the songs now being sung in worship across the spectrum of churches have come from the new churches. In the first two-thirds of the twentieth century there was very little hymn-writing but the century has ended with an outpouring of new hymns and songs, one of the expressions of new life in the church.

This year, upwards of 175,000 people in this country will be going on family holidays to Christian celebration and teaching events. Well over a quarter of a million people have been at least once in the last five years. This is another area of remarkable growth since the 1980s. First there was the historic Keswick Convention and centres such as Lee Abbey and Scargill House with their Christian communities. Then came Spring Harvest, taking over a holiday camp for a week. Spring Harvest is now spread over three weeks at three holiday centres and draws over 70,000 people a year. There are also Easter People, Stoneleigh, New Wine, Soul Survivor, Greenbelt Christian arts festival and a host of other events.

Leading figures in this resurgence have themselves come from the roots. Between them they have touched the hearts and lives of hundreds of thousands of people. They have been the means of leading many into personal commitment to Christ and have been used to encourage and strengthen the faith of many more, whose Christian discipleship, witness and service have deepened.

What kind of people are they? What is their background? There are 17 of them featured in this book and there are, of course, others. Of those featured here there are six Anglicans, four from the new churches, three Pentecostalists, two Baptists, a Salvationist and a Methodist. Their service and influence however extend beyond any boundaries of denomination or stream. They are servants of the whole church. We are witnessing a resurgence in which the old demarcations are going as the wind of the Holy Spirit blows through them.

With one or two exceptions, the people in this book are unknown to the public at large, but among Christians they are held in affection and esteem as men and women God has raised up for these times, to teach, challenge and inspire. There is a tendency for Christians to put such people on pedestals, to regard them as celebrities, as 'super Christians'. In fact they face problems, personal crises and temptations just as all Christians do. Their prominence puts them in an even more exposed position. Those who are in the forefront of spiritual warfare can expect to come under attack. As I have prepared this book I have covered each of them in prayer because I know how easily they might fall. They need the support of all of us in their continuing ministries, in their own walk with the Lord and in their family life.

Interviews can be a sequence of questions and answers. In some, the interviewer weaves his or her own pattern around the interview, perhaps even slanting it. What I have done is have a relaxed conversation with each person, encouraging them to speak freely about their childhood, their coming to faith and their spiritual journey, including the setbacks and hard lessons as well as the progress. The whole transcript has then been pruned, but with sensitive editing, and checked back with the person concerned. After setting the scene at the start of each chapter, I have edited myself out, apart from occasional brief summarising. The effect I have tried to achieve is as if the person were sitting opposite you, the reader, and telling you their story. So come inside, and meet each one.

Wallace Boulton

1

GRAHAM KENDRICK

BLAZE, SPIRIT, BLAZE, SET OUR HEARTS ON FIRE

Graham Kendrick was casually dressed when we met in a comparatively quiet corner of the lounge in a Croydon hotel, and I found him natural and modest as he talked of his life and his music. He was born in Northamptonshire, where his father was a Baptist minister. He has been led into a far bigger musical ministry than he could ever have imagined. Millions around the world have sung his worship songs, his songs proclaiming key aspects of Christian thought and his songs articulating compassion and a desire for justice.

When I rang his office some time afterwards the reply was, 'He's in Moscow today.' He is certainly much in demand around the world. When we met he had just returned from a tour of south-east Asia. How did it all begin? I asked him first about his childhood in the manse.

We moved from Blisworth in Northamptonshire when I was six or seven years old to Laindon in Essex, then when I was thirteen to Putney in London. I didn't find these moves too disruptive; it was a happy childhood and I remember being very content.

I was the third of four children. There was a
moment when I was only about five or six which
left a strong impression on me. My mother was
reading a bedtime story to the three oldest of us.
The story explained the gospel. When she closed
the book she asked us if we wanted to invite Jesus
into our hearts and to give our lives over to him.

I decided that I would, and I prayed a prayer, as
she suggested, in my own way, in my own words.
I can still remember a sudden sense of surprise, a
feeling that something important had happened. It
was the first time I had made a conscious decision.
I think the other two children responded in some
way but I am not sure that they would necessarily
remember that moment as I do. In any case, I am
sure that for all of us it was just one milestone in
faith, although for me it was a major one.

When I was about eleven we were told at
church that we should tell others about our faith. I
remember being with my best friend at school and
opening my mouth to try to do that but then I did-
n't know quite what to say; I couldn't find words
of my own to communicate my faith to someone
else.

I think that for any child who is brought up in a
Christian environment, much of it is just 'there'
and accepted. The way my parents lived com-
mended their faith and certainly in my case helped
me to make it my own.

When I was a teenager, however, I became cynical about the way things were in the church. It
seemed to belong to my parents' generation, a culturally different one. I was not relating to it and
was prompted to find what an authentic faith

should mean for young people. Much of my early songwriting was an attempt to take the church into the next generation.

When I was about fifteen I took an interest in the guitar and decided to teach myself. This was after an initial abortive attempt to learn to play the piano. At that time Christian coffee bars were a popular means of evangelism and there were Christian music groups playing there. So my older brother and sister and I, and a couple of friends, formed a band. We began by using other people's songs. I didn't like them very much so I decided to write some of my own and became the band's main writer.

Sadly, Graham's sister Gillian died of cancer in 1989. His older brother Peter joined the London City Mission and now visits schools and runs an educational resources centre for teachers. Graham went to teacher training college . . .

This was a decision I made after a 'gap year' in which I had been a student teacher at a local prep school, teaching art and geography to nine- and ten-year-olds and taking them for sport. I thoroughly enjoyed it and it was a good experience for me in front of a class.

When I went to the college I pursued an interest in the contemporary folk music of the day, sold my electric guitar and got an acoustic guitar. I began to write more folk-style songs, which were influenced by people like Paul Simon. At that time I was trying to be a bit of a poet and an artist, free to write about anything, but also recognising that it was a good communication medium to my own generation.

That really began my career, doing concerts where I would sing my songs and talk about the gospel. I would write songs about biblical characters, updating and dramatising the whole story. It was very different from the music I was writing later.

In the early 1970s I began to be exposed to some of the then new praise and worship choruses which were coming into the country or being written here. Looking back, it was a watershed. I was working with Clive Calver, who was at that time leading Youth for Christ and who later became general director of the Evangelical Alliance.

I was being asked to lead some of the worship choruses of the day. I complained to Clive that these songs were simplistic, not very interesting and a bit shallow, although I couldn't deny that there was an anointing of the Holy Spirit in them. He said, 'Rather than complain about them, you're a songwriter, you do better!' I had no real motivation at the time to write songs of that kind, so he actually goaded me into writing some.

It was during a mission in Wolverhampton, when Graham was part of the evangelistic team there with Clive Calver, that he met Jill, who was to become his wife. She has a Methodist background; her grandfather was a Methodist local preacher. They now have four daughters, aged twenty, seventeen, fifteen and ten.

It's a very busy and lively household. I would describe Jill as multi-tasked. She trained with the National Health Service as an administrator and is now responsible for the Make Way Music office which looks after the publishing of my songs, the contract side and the itinerary. At first the office was in our garage but we have recently moved it out to nearby accommodation where we now have two staff.

* * * * *

When I qualified at the end of my three years at college I decided to take a year off, pursuing the musical activities and concerts. One thing led to another and, all these years later, I still haven't got a proper job!

One of the songs I wrote after Clive Calver's challenge was 'Jesus, stand among us'. At that time there was no publishing infrastructure for worship songs. People would simply turn up to meetings with a notebook, take down the words and afterwards ask you what the chords were. They would then reproduce the song, usually slightly altered, at their meeting on the next Sunday.

So that song got on the grapevine and I occasionally began to write worship songs. Most of these, however, were used only in our own small circle until several years later, when Geoff Shearn, then at Kingsway Music, persuaded me to record a selection of them on an album entitled *Jesus stand among us*. It quickly outsold my contemporary releases. To be honest, I was not too happy about it because I saw myself as an 'artist' and not as a worship leader.

Then Spring Harvest began. Because Youth for Christ was one of the sponsors, and I was its musical director, I was asked to lead worship. Then of course there was a demand for new songs.

Spring Harvest, and the other Bible weeks at the time, became a platform for new writers, many of whom are established now, like Chris Bowater and Dave Fellingham. The Bible weeks popularised songs and stimulated the writing of more songs. There was a hunger for new songs.

I wondered how Graham finds the inspiration for a new song. Does he sit down and think about it or does an idea come into his head unexpectedly?

Ideas come in many ways. Yes, occasionally there will be a spontaneous idea, most likely in a time of worship. There have been times when I have begun a song on the spot and tried it out instantly: 'Try this everybody!' Those songs would be quite brief and usually need a fair amount of work afterwards to take them further. But a live worship session will often bring forth at least a seed idea. I will also sit down with the intention of writing a song on a particular subject.

Over the years Graham has received requests from organisations and individuals to write songs for specific occasions and events. Among those he has written for are Care for the Family, Tearfund, Church Army, Ichthus Christian Fellowship, CARE and The Children's Society.

Tearfund, for example, asked me to write a song for its 25th anniversary. I asked for some starting points: key scriptures and some videos of the work. I immersed myself in the subject. One of the notes I jotted down as I was brainstorming became a starting point. I built from there and eventually completed the song 'Beauty for brokenness'. I don't think I have ever spent so long working on a song. The subject was a great challenge.

I have a music room at home and I normally shut myself away there when I am working on a song. It's at the 'quiet' end of the house, but with four children I am not sure that there is any such thing. Late at night, when everyone else has gone to bed, is often good working time.

I have on occasions gone away, borrowing someone's weekend cottage. Getting right away can be good, because of the need to be completely immersed, to get really into the creative mood. I find unbroken concentration for a long spell very difficult to attain.

I could easily spend at least a day on a verse of a song, getting it right. The time I spent on the Tearfund song would add up to two or three weeks' solid work. A lot gets crossed out or thrown away. Other people are possibly much quicker, but I tend to be slow and quite laborious. If it's just a four-line chorus, that would probably come together fairly quickly, but not a five-verse hymn plus a chorus, on a different theme. A doctrinal subject needs to be treated very carefully.

For someone who is 'giving out' so much, are there opportunities for 'taking in'; for learning and thinking about theological issues?

Yes there are. I am a member of the leadership team of the Ichthus Christian Fellowship. It's very stimulating, with folk like Roger and Faith Forster who are very alive and alert in doctrine, theology and church practice, and Bible teachers like Ken McGreavy. Being part of a living, growing, worshipping church is very important to me.

Often I feel that my role is simply to express what God is doing in the church; to capture the mood or the direction we are taking; to take some relevant truths and put them into a song that everyone can sing. Roger and Faith and other members of the leadership team provide very valuable input into the whole process.

Graham has been very involved from the start with March for Jesus. He and his friends Roger Forster, Gerald Coates and Lynn Green were the founders of what has become a worldwide movement. The first march was in London in 1985, when Graham began writing some songs especially for when the church took to the streets.

When March for Jesus went global I had a crazy idea of being at the start of two marches on the same day, one in Western Samoa and one in New Zealand, by travelling across the international dateline. The BBC used its overseas correspondents and film crews to produce a programme from different locations and the result was a memorable *Songs of Praise*.

People's lives are being changed by the gospel message and they want to celebrate its life-changing truths and express their experience in thanks and praise. Through the centuries this has been done through the popular music of the day. Many of the traditional hymns we venerate as 'quality' music were originally sung to popular tavern tunes. Charles Wesley was criticised for borrowing ideas from the operettas of the day. Hymn writers have often been in the forefront of their culture. What I personally like to see is the best of the old and the best of the new used side by side.

There is a need to reflect many different styles, particularly in cities. Worship is becoming more and more the meeting point of the international Christian community. Perhaps it's easiest for us to come together at different levels in the context of worship. If we just sat down to discuss our differences and our variations in doctrine and church practice, we wouldn't get very far.

Because worship is a spiritual activity and a spiritual experience, we begin to enjoy spiritual unity. Perhaps the devil can test worship and wants to make it a divisive issue because it is potentially the most unifying action, whether it's in our local church or in the international community. So that's why it's contested.

When we put Christ in the centre, and begin to worship him, he becomes our common ground and our differences start to melt away.

2

NICKY GUMBEL

'WE ARE CERTAINLY SEEING NEW LIFE'

Past London's Hyde Park Corner and along Brompton Road, beyond Harrods and across the road, is the drive leading to what has become known far and wide simply as 'HTB' – Holy Trinity Brompton, a church at the forefront of renewal and the nerve centre of the Alpha courses for which 6,488 churches in the UK are now registered. Worldwide the figure has reached 11,656, in 78 countries.

At the heart of Alpha is Nicky Gumbel, who runs the courses at HTB where it all began. When I met him, there had been 650 people at an Alpha supper in the church the night before. Over 1,100 people had accepted invitations so the event was spread over two evenings. Many people are won for Christ through the Alpha courses, then they invite their friends to the next supper and these friends are in turn invited to the next course. The number of Christians keeps multiplying.

I met Nicky Gumbel in the subterranean brick-arched offices, which are a hive of activity. We walked across to the other church building, alongside what looked like a village green, an unexpected sight in the middle of Knightsbridge. In this block there were more staff busily engaged.

When we found a free space, Nicky Gumbel told me

*how instead of continuing his career as a barrister, he
had been ordained and had come to HTB as a curate. He
had no idea then what lay in store . . .*

I was born in London, brought up actually within
the parish here. With both my parents barristers
and both my grandfathers barristers, it seemed
that the dye was cast for my career. Indeed, just
days after I was born my father agreed with a
member of a leading set of barristers' chambers
that I would one day be a 'pupil' there.

My father was a very private man but my
mother was involved in public life; she was a vice-
chairman of the former Greater London Council, a
JP and a lecturer. Neither of my parents was a
churchgoer, though we came once to the church, to
what we called 'midnight mass'.

My father married when he was forty-nine and
I was born in 1955, when he was fifty-two. That
made a difference, but it was a happy childhood.
My sister Elizabeth Anne is eighteen months older
than I am. I was sent to boarding school, to Eton,
where I quickly adjusted. I made many friends
there and I enjoyed the school sports. My wife and
I wouldn't however send our own children to
boarding school. For us it's been important to have
our children at home.

By the time I went to Trinity College,
Cambridge I was well on the way to achieving my
father's ambition for me. As for church, it played
no part in my life. I called myself, rather preten-
tiously, a logical determinist, with the idea that
everything is predetermined. Halfway through
my first year at Cambridge there was a week of

mission meetings led by David Macinnes. At the time I was sharing rooms with Nicky Lee, a friend from schooldays. He had been taken to the mission on the Saturday night, when I was at the Valentine's Ball. When Nicky got back he told me that he had become a Christian. I was horrified, particularly when he told me that he had agreed to go out to lunch with David Macinnes the following day. I thought he was going to be dragged into some cult. I told him that it could be dangerous, that he must have somebody with him. He was to bring David Macinnes back to lunch and then I could be with him and 'protect' him.

The next day I was amazed to find myself warming to this 'dangerous' visitor. He was such a gracious man. That night I went along to his meeting and when I came back I decided I would investigate whether there was anything in it. I dug out an old Bible which I still had from RE lessons at school and I read through Matthew, Mark, Luke and about halfway through John, until about 3 a.m.

I finished reading through the New Testament over the next two days and I knew I had to make a decision. I thought it would be the end of everything I enjoyed. I was eighteen, I had a lot of friends and I was having a wild social life. But I knew that what I had read was true. I went to see Jonathan Fletcher, the curate at the Round Church. He told me that if I became a Christian it would mean three things: I would have to give up everything I knew was wrong, I would have to be willing to be known as a Christian, and I would have to hand over the driving seat of my life to Christ.

I walked back across Great Court and I thought I would put this off to my death bed. The implications for my life were such that I thought it would be ruined. Then I sensed – and I think it was God speaking to me – that if I didn't do it then, I never would. So I simply said, 'Well yes, OK'. It was February 16th 1974 and at that moment everything clicked into place. Suddenly I understood what life was about. I found what I had been looking for unconsciously all my life.

A year earlier I had met Pippa, who was to become my wife. She had a friend she wanted to take to a nightclub of which I was a member. A mutual friend gave her my name, so we became friends. That was our sort of lifestyle at that stage. She became a Christian about six months after I did. It was nothing to do with me; in fact I think I rather put her off because she thought I had gone mad. But we then met up again, became engaged and were married in January 1978. It is very much a joint ministry. We have three children: sons aged nineteen and seventeen and a daughter of fourteen. They are very supportive and a great blessing.

After graduating Nicky returned to London to take his Bar exams and joined his local church – HTB. After qualifying, he worked as a barrister for six years. The workload continually increased and so did his involvement at HTB, where he became a lay pastor. Eventually he decided to offer for ordination.

The Gumbels moved to Oxford, where Nicky trained for ordination at Wycliffe Hall. When it came to seeking a curacy, he went to nine parishes and for one reason or another they all fell through. He began to think serious-

*ly about going back to work at the Bar. Then out of the
blue came an invitation to return to Holy Trinity
Brompton. The Bishop of Kensington gave permission
for him to be an extra member of the ordained staff
there. For four years he took on the youth group, ran a
pastorate, organised training courses and took charge of
the children's ministry. Then, in 1990, came Alpha . . .*

It had been started in 1977 as a four-week
course for new Christians by Charles Marnham,
who was then curate at HTB. It was held in his flat
and I had given a talk myself on one of the early
courses. Then another curate, John Irvine, took it
on and he developed it into a ten-week course and
weekend. My friend Nicky Lee then ran it for five
years and it began to attract people who were not
yet committed Christians. When I took over, the
emphasis had shifted in that direction. As it
became evangelistic it grew rapidly, so that by
May 1993 there were about 400 people coming
each time. Word got round and when we had our
first Alpha conference in that month it attracted
more than a thousand church leaders.

*The whole course at HTB was videoed to make it pos-
sible for people to hold small-group Alpha courses in
their homes. Many more Alpha conferences were
planned — all over the world — and Nicky Gumbel's
books, starting with* Questions of Life *and* Searching
Issues, *became Christian best-sellers. The national pro-
motional campaign, the Alpha Initiative, which ran in
the autumn of 1998, raised the public profile of the
Alpha course and attracted extensive media coverage.*

The Alpha Initiative exceeded our expectations
in three ways. The first was in the number of
churches that registered; it went up from 4,500 to

6,400. The second was in terms of unity: there were a great many groups of Christians from across the denominations who prayed together, uniting round a common goal of reaching people with the gospel. The third was in the number of unchurched people who came on the course. The aim of the initiative was to increase awareness of Alpha throughout the country and to make it easier for people to invite their friends. Our survey of churches showed that the average number of people on each course doubled as a result of the Initiative.

If you run an Alpha course – certainly the way we run it here and encourage other churches to run it – you should expect people to have a powerful experience of the Holy Spirit during the course, in whatever way is applicable to that particular church. That inevitably leads to renewal. Similarly, if a church has been touched by the Spirit of God, 'you will be my witnesses', as Jesus said. This need not be through the Alpha course, it may be through another way, but many churches are finding that the Alpha course is an ideal model for them to use for evangelism.

Everybody is resisting using the term 'revival' but it depends how revival is being defined. One definition is 'bringing new life'. We are certainly seeing new life coming into the church and people outside the church being affected. Our experience here, and the reports we get back from the courses round the country, is that people are coming to faith in Christ, being filled with the Holy Spirit, getting excited about Jesus and telling their friends. More and more people are getting converted. God is pouring out his love on people of all ages.

I believe it is important always to keep in view the supreme goal, which is that God's name is honoured and that his kingdom comes. That must mean keeping evangelism to the fore.

The comment has been made that there has generally been little emphasis on repentance, but we have seen many, many instances of repentance. People are leaving behind the old life because they have seen something better. We have seen a lot of weeping over past sins. One woman wept for an hour over an abortion she had had eighteen years previously. We have seen people crying out, 'I repent of my sins, I repent of my sins.'

It is a wonderful kind of repentance. It's like the repentance of the prodigal son: he turned round, changed his mind and his father welcomed him with open arms. There was joy and celebration. That is what we are seeing. Repentance is very positive, as it is in the New Testament. People are changing their lifestyle because they don't want to lose that new relationship with God.

The movement of the Holy Spirit brings churches together. He is doing that right across the denominations and within the traditions. Locally we have always worked with all the denominations and all the Alpha conferences go right across the board. We are seeing Roman Catholics involved now, as well as Anglicans, Methodists, Baptists, United Reformed and members of new churches. Nobody is suspicious of anybody else. Everyone is working together and I believe that is what the Spirit achieves. The Spirit brings unity to the church. A disunited church, squabbling and criticising, makes it very hard for the world to believe.

If the church just gets caught up with itself, that is very sad. We are seeing, thankfully, a new concentration on evangelism. As on the day of Pentecost, when people are filled with the Holy Spirit they want to spread the message. That is surely a mark of the work of the Spirit. We are not doing anything differently from the way we have done it before. The only difference is that we are seeing people having more powerful experiences of God. He is sovereignly choosing to pour out his love on the church and on individuals. We are simply praying for God's Spirit to come.

Jesus said, 'How much more will your Father in heaven give the Holy Spirit to all who ask?' That is all we are doing. We are asking him to give the Holy Spirit: more of his Spirit to his people. And we are seeing him do it.

3

J JOHN

'THERE WERE SO MANY DOORS OF OPPORTUNITY'

My meeting with J John took me to leafy Metroland, to Chorleywood, just into Hertfordshire from outer suburbia. From the quiet shopping street I turned into Quickley Lane, which must be the road with more connections with renewal than any other. Among its residents are Mark and Alie Stibbe, Barry and Mary Kissell and J John and his wife Killy, while close by lives Mike Pilavachi, leader of Soul Survivor. On one side of the road is St Andrew's, a church at the forefront of renewal.

I was warmly greeted by J John, whose heart is so much in evangelism. His love of people, his naturalness and humour have helped to communicate the gospel effectively to all kinds of people in many different situations. As he talked, however, I soon discovered that life has not been all sunshine for this cheerful servant of the Lord.

My parents were Greek Cypriots. My Greek name is Iouannes Iouannou – John, son of John, though John was actually my grandfather's name, such is Greek naming. My brother was born in Cyprus but I was born in London, in 1958. Many people emigrated from Cyprus after the war there in the fifties and my parents took the opportunity to come to England. But they found it difficult with two children in a foreign country not knowing the language. So my grandmother took me and my brother back to Cyprus for three years.

When we came back to England and I started school I hardly knew a word of English. My parents spoke to me only in Greek at home. I struggled to survive at school and it took a long, long time to catch up. Meanwhile my father had become the owner of a restaurant in London. He worked very hard, as many people from ethnic groups do. They work long hours because they are high achievers and want the next generation to progress and be academically and financially better off. This put pressure on me. My parents wanted me to go to university and become a professional – doctor, lawyer, something like that with stature in a worldly sense.

The extended family unit was so strong that there was not much opportunity to mix with others; I really only had my cousins to play with as a child. My parents, like most Greeks, were Greek Orthodox. For them it was part of the culture. They went to church at Christmas and Easter but there was no religious expression within their everyday life.

I quite enjoyed senior school but the pressure to succeed from my parents was even greater. A 'B' mark was not good enough; it had to be an 'A'. If it was 'A' it was not good enough unless I was first in the class. I felt a failure because I often fell short of those standards. My brother was more able, academically and at sport, so he fared better. He went on to university and is now head of business studies at a school. He is also a Christian.

I went from school to Hendon sixth-form college, where I did A-level psychology, sociology and biology. It was there that my whole life changed. During my first week there I met Andy Economides, a Greek Cypriot who was doing a different course. Over about five months he built a bridge from him to me and, when the bridge was built, Jesus Christ walked over it. It was like a light had come on. Andy told me about the cross; he explained it all to me.

What clinched it was when he showed me Revelation 3:20. I know some people may say this verse is taken out of context, but somehow it still works. Jesus stands at the door and knocks and if you open the door he will come in. Andy asked me if I had opened the door. He said, 'If I was knocking on your front door and you didn't answer, how long do you think I would wait before I went away? It's not that Jesus stops knocking, it's that you won't hear the knock.' I went home that night and opened the door to Jesus.

What followed was an indication that J John's calling would be as an evangelist: the next day he led a fellow student to the Lord, and another a couple of days later. He joined Andy Economides' church – Christ Church in North Finchley – where there was a strong Christian youth group with about 70 members. They sang pre-Kendrick choruses, had Bible studies and talks and went out on evangelism on Saturdays.

At home, however, J John's parents strongly disapproved of what was happening.

My mother said I was brainwashed and I said, 'Mother, my brain *has* been washed.' They got the Greek Orthodox bishop to come and see me, and he asked what had happened to me. I didn't yet know the Bible very well, although I was beginning to get acquainted with it. I took the Greek Bible and I found passages in the Scripture and described my experience. The bishop was stunned and said it was amazing. He told my parents, 'Your son has the favour of God upon him.' This did nothing to relieve my parents' hostility and they insisted that he carried out an 'exorcism' on me at his church. During the exorcism, in Greek, my father fell on the floor sick and my mother accused me, saying that demons in me had attacked him.

Things got worse at home. I came home one day to find that my mother had torn up and burnt all my Christian books: biographies as well as the Bible. My parents became really violent towards me and it got so bad that I had to leave home. I did psychiatric nursing, for which I had just enough qualifications. This provided me with accommodation, a salary and study course. I knew this was temporary because what I really wanted to study was theology. I had a hunger and thirst for knowledge of God.

I think I was baptised in the Spirit at my conversion, and then a couple of weeks later I had another incredible experience and from then on spoke in tongues. I was reading the Bible for a couple of hours a day and was going through it in weeks, from cover to cover.

I nursed for just over a year, before going to St

John's College, Nottingham. I had left home but it was when I was baptised that my parents said, 'You're dead, we never want to see you again.' For about three years I never saw them, then when I did see them again, things just got worse. Culture is very strong and for my parents it was not just a question of a religious change but of renouncing my Greekness. The next great crisis was when I rang them to tell them I was going to get married and that was awful.

Completing his studies at St John's College, J John realised that ordination was not for him. His role was to be an evangelist. After a spell at the Christian Renewal Centre in Rostrevor he was invited to join the staff of St Nicholas', Nottingham, working with David and Joyce Huggett and the team there as director of evangelism.

I linked up with Eric Delve as well and became an assistant on his missions. I would do six or eight missions a year with him and the rest of the time I had this role at St Nicholas'. I had days of not really knowing how to speak or preach but I had lots of enthusiasm and God used it. People came to faith and things happened. I learned a lot.

My parents blamed me initially for making my brother a Christian, but because he is a teacher it carried more status. They would have nothing to do with Killy, who became my wife. She comes from generations of evangelists. Killy's father is Michael Rees, a clergyman. Her maternal grandparents were missionaries in Burma and her paternal grandfather was the evangelist Dick Rees, whose brother Tom filled the Royal Albert Hall for evangelistic rallies in the fifties. I am a first generation evangelical Christian and I was marrying into this Christian stock.

I met Killy when I was taking a mission at
Cambridge with about fifty-five students, reaching thousands of overseas students. Killy was on
vacation from college and had 'shelved'
Christianity at the time. I persuaded her to come
and hear me speak and she came forward at the
end. She was the first one to the front and she
recommitted her life to Christ. We became friends
and that friendship later developed.

When we got married Killy had a job in cater-
ing. In fact, she was supporting me. Then she travelled with me. We went to Australia twice – with a
baby. Those were days of preaching three times a
day, sleeping, then travelling somewhere else and
preaching again. We went to Greece and Canada
as well. Tours like that lasted for over two months.

We now have three sons – Michael, Simon and
Benjamin – and Killy is a full-time mother and
wife. I have learned the rhythm of knowing when
to be at home and when to travel less and be more
effective. We relax together; we are a fun family.
We love to watch a film together and if I am at
home on a Friday night, it is video, pizza and coke.
We love any holidays and Killy and I try to play
golf once a week on my day off.

* * * * *

After three years at St Nicholas' I could not believe
how many doors of opportunity were opening. I
knew I could not respond and still do a good job at
St Nicholas'. That is when the Philo Trust was created as a support group for my ministry. In the

early days there was no money – I did not even
have a bank account.

*As J John's ministry, nationally and internationally,
has grown, the Philo Trust has grown to keep pace with
it.*

It now has several full-time and part-time staff
so the budget is quite big. But even after nearly
eighteen years we require 76 per cent of our
income to come in through gifts. We have no
assets; Philo Trust does not own any offices or anything.

We had been in Nottingham for some years
when St Andrew's, Chorleywood, invited us to
relocate our family and our ministry here. Mark
Stibbe, the vicar, and I have been prayer partners
for five years. Killy and I sought the Lord over the
move and knew, 'Yes, this is right.' We are now living in a place that is more of a community than a
city. St Andrew's is very supportive and I sense
that it is important that we are near London for
our involvement in the next couple of years.

I have broken the addiction to the word 'yes'; I
get about a hundred requests a month and cannot
say yes to them all. I meet regularly with the
trustees of the Philo Trust. We are sensing what we
should focus on and where the priorities lie.
Discerning what God wants to be done is the crux
point.

I think the spiritual climate is warming more
and more. I find that people are more open than I
have ever known. I would love to see the church
working together more for the sake of the gospel,
because ultimately it is the gospel that will change
the nation. I feel that for me as an evangelist the

past seventeen years have been an apprenticeship.
Even though I have taken 179 missions in twenty-
three countries and written a few books, I feel it
has been but a preparation for what lies ahead.

I am mentor to six young evangelists. I am
investing in the next generation, using my influence and connections to help others, so that they
do not need seventeen years to have the access I
have.

4

STEVE CHALKE

DIXON ROAD WILL ALWAYS BE REMEMBERED

I left Waterloo East station against a tide of commuters scurrying for their trains home and began a brisk walk at dusk along the side streets towards the latest quarters of the Oasis Trust and Oasis Media. There I was meeting Steve Chalke, a man with a heart for evangelism whose calling has taken him into enterprising Christian social action as well as into the media.

My walk through Southwark took me past the imposing shell of a new station on the Jubilee Line extension, workshops, car lots, small businesses, blocks of housing-trust dwellings, pubs, petrol stations, cafés and busy junctions until I came, amid this conglomeration of workaday London, to the corner block in Southwark Bridge Road occupied by Oasis. On the second floor the young staff of Oasis Media were preparing to go home, but in his inner office Steve Chalke was relaxed and unhurried as I prompted him to talk about his life and calling.

I was born and brought up in South Norwood in south-east London. My mother is English and my father is Anglo-Indian. I have one brother and two sisters; I am the oldest and we go down in stages

of two years. Our house was in a road off
Whitehorse Lane, which is just by the Crystal
Palace football ground. When I was a boy I could
see half the match for nothing through the bed-
room window but then the club built a new stand
and that blocked the view.

My parents are both Christians. They went to
the local Baptist church because the nearest
Anglican church was spiritually dead at the time,
though now it is a large flourishing church. My
mother liked the Holmesdale Baptist Church
because it had a meeting on Wednesday afternoons for young mothers. This ran for many years;
in fact they were still called 'the young wives'
when they had reached their sixties.

I went to that church throughout my childhood,
rebelled against it, stopped going and then in my
teens went back because there was a girl there I
liked called Mary Hooper. I had to go to the
Saturday night youth club to see her and it was
through that eventually that I became a Christian.
People often ask me now why I am a Baptist and
not an Anglican or in one of the new churches.
They are looking for some theological reason, but
it is actually because Mary Hooper went to the
Baptist youth club.

When I was fourteen or fifteen, students from
Spurgeon's College ran a week of special events at
the youth club. Graham Kendrick, who was at
teacher training college at the time, came and sang
each evening. My job was to sell the Cokes. On the
Friday night one of the student team, Ken
Humphreys, said to me, 'You know, Steve, lots of
kids have come in and it's a shame that they are

wandering out afterwards and have not become Christians.' I sympathetically replied, 'Yes, it's an awful shame.' He then looked at me, pointed at me and said, 'You are in exactly the same boat as they are.' He then marched out.

On my way home I wandered thoughtfully along Dixon Road realising that what he had said was true. I had known what the gospel was. It wasn't that I had rejected being a Christian, it was just that I had never really thought about it. I then decided that if God created me, gave me life, and Jesus died on the cross for me, then I had to give my life back. That was it really. It takes about five minutes to walk up Dixon Road and by the time I reached the top I had decided that when I grew up I would spend my life telling people about Jesus and I would start a hostel, a hospital and a school for the poor and homeless. The Oasis Trust has been the vehicle from which to deliver these things.

When I told my minister that I had become a Christian he didn't believe me. I had a friend, Keith, who became a Christian at about the same time. A few months later he was baptised but the minister refused to baptise me. It took me a year to convince him. When I had completed my A-levels I wanted to become a student at Spurgeon's College. I had to go there and apply for a place, putting my case in front of the whole college council, which was about forty-strong, in one of the lecture theatres.

At the end, the vice-principal led me into the library and said, 'You've really impressed us today, Steve, and so we are going to send you away for a year, to Gravesend.' If I succeeded in completing the year successfully, Spurgeon's College would accept me as a student the following year. I just managed to hold back tears at the thought of being sent to this place I had hardly heard of rather than being admitted to the college. I was just twenty and they thought that the year's experience would do me good.

I was very miserable when I went off to Gravesend but actually loved the year I had there helping the minister, David Beer. Looking back now I can see how all the bits of my life have fallen into place in a way that has been almost totally dependent on my spending that year in Gravesend. If I had not done so, Oasis Trust would not exist, nor would Oasis Media and I would not have become involved in television.

David Beer revealed to me much later that Spurgeon's had told him when I went to spend my year with him that he was to get rid of my South London accent and get me sorted out, but he had decided to leave me as I was. When I went to college I was just from a different social background, very working class; my dad worked on the railway. I recall going on preaching engagements from the college, being invited to lunch with the church secretary and sitting at the lunch table being confused by all the cutlery. I found the whole experience of college, its culture, and the study and ethics of the place, incredible.

Each year I was summoned to the principal's office. Dr Raymond Brown was a friend to me and he would say, 'Steve, if you keep on like this you will never pass any exams.' I was always involved in lots of evangelistic projects I had set up. I did always manage, however, to scrape through the exams, just about. I was very involved in youth work and that was also frowned on. One of the tutors said to me, 'You are receiving a real theological education here. Don't waste it on teenagers.' On another occasion I was told, 'You are being given four years of theological training. Don't blow it on becoming an evangelist. You are being trained to pastor people and nurture the church.'

The attitude at that time seemed to be that anyone could do evangelism. That's been part of the problem with the church in this country. We have had churches led by pastors but we have not trained evangelists. In the Baptist Church a century ago there were as many accredited evangelists holding office as there were pastors, but that breed died out altogether. The apostle Paul spoke of apostles, prophets, evangelists and pastors and teachers. Most churches have dropped at least some of them. Within the Baptist denomination, if you are a pastor or teacher that's fine. If you were an evangelist you were always on the edge but you were rescued by your ability to pastor as well. There are men older than I am who opted out of the Baptist Church because they found there was no place for an evangelist.

I married Cornelia just before my last year at Spurgeon's College. I had known her since I was about twelve at Holmesdale Baptist Church. She also made a commitment to Christ but at one point went off on a different track. I stayed involved with the Christian faith because of a great friend of

mine, Steve Flashman. He was at Spurgeon's
College at the time and asked me to join his evangelistic band. He taught me to play the bass guitar
and I went out on youth weekends and played in
church services and concerts. He also encouraged
me to speak on these occasions. It was a valuable
training ground for me. Just as important was that
it kept me out of harm's way at the age of sixteen
or seventeen when friends were at parties, being
drunk and getting into all sorts of things they later
regretted.

When I returned from Gravesend I met
Cornelia again. She recommitted herself to Christ,
then some time later we started to go out together,
became engaged and married. We now have four
children: Emily is sixteen, David fifteen, Abigail
twelve and Joshua ten. The Lord has blessed us
with our children, they are great. The biggest ten-
sion for me is how to balance family life with
working life, with my increasing responsibilities
and so many staff in this country. I try hard to
carve out time and my principle is that I go home
and work as hard at being a husband and father as
I do at being the boss when I am at Oasis or
involved in television.

I have stopped travelling as much I used to. I
rarely speak in churches on a Saturday or Sunday
now as that means being away for a whole weekend. I constantly try to find ways of doing things
with each of the children on their own. Since we
have had children Cornelia has never worked outside the home. We felt this was really important,
especially because I am away from time to time. It
was a tough decision to make because there is only

one income and there are things you can't afford to buy and places you can't afford to go. But actually you are investing in your children in a way that you wouldn't otherwise be able to do. Every couple has to make their own decision on this.

When I finished at Spurgeon's College, David Beer had moved on from Gravesend to Tonbridge and he invited me to be his assistant minister. I worked alongside David there for five years. It is one of the largest Baptist churches in the country and attached to it were 200 to 300 teenagers. I was the minister responsible for the youth and children's work and there were sixty or seventy people involved in running it.

It was out of Tonbridge Baptist Church that the Oasis Trust was born in my final year there. Church members who had been appointed as my support group helped me to establish it. I still worked as an evangelist but also embarked on setting up a hostel, clearly remembering the commitment I had made to the Lord while walking along Dixon Road years earlier.

The first Oasis hostel was established in Peckham in south-east London and is still operating. The Oasis Trust now runs other hostels, orphanages, clinics, a hospital, employment projects, training schemes and drop-in centres, and mobilises volunteer teams for various assignments, not only in this country but in India, Brazil, various parts of Africa, France and Portugal. Meanwhile opportunities were developing for Steve in television.

At an evangelists' conference I was leading a Communion service and afterwards Gerald Coates came to me and gave me a little badge, of a microphone. He said, 'I wear this badge because I believe God has called me to be a spokesman to this nation. I believe God is calling you to be that spokesman. Wear this badge as a sign of that calling.' This message was confirmed, though in different terminology, by another friend, Ken Costa.

I am not someone who hears from God very clearly and I would find it hard to write on guidance, but there have been two occasions when I have felt that God communicated distinctly with me. One was when I became a Christian walking up Dixon Road and the second was through what I have just described.

In 1990, I had been featured in a BBC 2 documentary series on people's jobs. There were programmes on a teacher, a fireman, a lawyer and a salesman. I was included in the series as an evangelist. I was followed around for six months in the making of the programme. It was an interesting experience and I learned a great deal from it.

It was through David Beer however that I became a television presenter. He had moved on from Tonbridge to Frinton and had become an adviser to Anglia Television. Anglia won a contract to provide religious programmes, including a youth slot, for the ITV network on Sunday mornings. David put Anglia in touch with me and for eight weeks I presented the youth slot in the series. The topics included fashion, homelessness and war. While I was doing these, the GMTV breakfast programme asked me to be involved and then the BBC invited me to do some *Songs of Praise* programmes, which I still do occasionally. I am also about to do another series for Anglia.

Oasis Media is quite separate from the Oasis Trust. It is a production company making television programmes. We have had commissions from the BBC and ITV and hope to get many more. We also work with Christian agencies such as Tearfund, helping them to relate their message to secular media. We do media coaching, as there are many Christians with important things to say on specific issues and they need to be put forward for the opportunity.

My goal in Oasis has always been to inspire and train others to get on with the job. Instead of seeing the media as a frightening beast to stay clear of, each local church needs to engage with it; to be involved. The church must once more be the hub of its local community and not only move into the media but move back into education, into housing, into entertainment, into every part of life. That's my vision and that's what both Oasis Trust and Oasis Media are all about.

5

JANE GRAYSHON
WHEN THE HANGING ON IS REALLY HARD

'Jane has been resting,' said Matthew Grayshon as he opened the door of the vicarage at Hanwell in west London. 'Last week was bad but she has been better this week. She will be down in a minute.' Popular author and speaker Jane Grayshon has lived with pain for years. She had recently come through a risky operation.

It seemed very peaceful in the vicarage study, with a large desk along one side and a chaise-longue catching the sunlight in front of the widows. Jane came in, took off her shoes and reclined comfortably on the chaise-longue for our conversation. She looked rather pale but otherwise there was little indication of her suffering. Indeed she was chirpy throughout and there were often flashes of the playful humour that marked The (Slightly edited) Confessions of a Vicar's Wife, *one of the two lighter books she has written as well as* A Pathway Through Pain *and* Treasures of Darkness. *She looked relaxed, so it seemed not too intrusive to ask straightaway about the operation. Was it successful?*

No, it wasn't. I made a very good recovery at first and for three weeks I was very much better. But the episodes of being unwell have kept coming back. It's a profound disappointment. I am very up and down; I have times of pain when I am confined to bed and on morphine every four to six hours, which is hard to live through. This tends to last for three or four days, then I have about the same length of time being better.

I don't know what the future holds. I still hope I am going to get better from one of these episodes and not have any more. It's the hanging on, not knowing, that is really hard: not knowing why it happens; not knowing what God is saying. It has convinced me that I never want to be the kind of Christian who talks as if knowing all the answers.

A lot of my writing and speaking is for people who have been puzzled by God and can't understand why God hasn't done the miracle they asked for. I suppose God is keeping alive in me the puzzlement and the confusion, and stopping me ever being glib. So that has to be good.

People around the parish have been extremely supportive and appreciative of everything that I have done, or done with Matthew. My GP called today to bring a chocolate cake she had made.

Jane Grayshon was born in Birkenhead on Merseyside, the third child of four.

It was a pretty strict Christian home so we were never allowed to do anything on a Sunday except read. It was a very happy childhood, all the way through. I can't remember a time when I was not a Christian. I remember when I was six praying and asking God to speak to me. My prayers were what people now call 'renewed'. I was surprised that God was speaking to me, that he was putting thoughts into my head, as I prayed that he would.

Although I was only six I can remember where I was walking when this happened. It was really the beginning of my walk with the Lord. I began reading my Bible and praying every day. I eventually settled on a church where many of my school friends went. It was very lively and the vicar was a brilliant preacher. I went to the midweek Bible teaching sessions, which were a sound grounding for me.

In the sixth form at school I helped to lead the Christian Union. I loved the school and I am still in contact with some of the teachers. My parents were very supportive of me, although there was an element of disappointment that I could have done more with my brain. My mother particularly would have liked me to have gone to university, but they knew I wanted to be a nurse, and even a missionary nurse. I went off to Edinburgh to train when I was eighteen.

Jane's mischievous sense of humour comes to the fore when she describes 'the strategic bit' a year earlier, when the exchange of greetings in 'the peace' was introduced at church.

There was a dishy man and you just had to make sure that you were sitting behind him. The best bit was when he was engineering to sit just in front of me. He was seven years older than I was; he was a teacher in Birkenhead, while I was still at school. I used to hitch my skirt to mini-skirt level to catch his eye. The shameful things we do! I would walk to school the way I knew he would be driving to his school so that he would happen to see me and we could wave to each other.

His name was Matthew Grayshon.

When I went up to Edinburgh I was hotly pursued by Matthew. He asked me to marry him when I had only just left home. I was nineteen then. It took some time to say yes. When I did, he moved to Edinburgh and we married at the end of my second year. I was twenty, a young bride, but we were very happy. I was just sure that he was the right man for me.

We had a flat in Edinburgh and joined St Thomas' Church. I finished my training and became a staff nurse. We led a church group for students. We were both adventurous and the idea of mission service abroad was there, but it didn't predominate. We rather thought of Matthew being a headmaster – with me as the school matron.

It all changed when we went on holiday to Iona the following year. We joined the fellowship meetings of a Church of Scotland group at the abbey. During those three days Matthew realised that his calling was to be a minister. He passed the selection board for ordination training. I had started my midwifery training when we moved to Nottingham, to St John's College. We were very happy there and made many friends. Matthew had to do a minimum of two years' training but extended it to four: he said that if there was more to learn he would rather learn it first than on the job.

I was working, doing midwifery as research. I had patients in the clinical area, but I was using my brain in the university department of obstetrics and gynaecology. I was working with the professor and two consultants – a job that I thoroughly enjoyed.

Matthew joined a college mission to Beverley and, just as he had started to look for a curacy, he was asked to be curate at Beverley Minster. The choice came very easily.

Jane was first ill in Edinburgh, after having her appendix removed.

I was very, very ill for six weeks. They operated again and found that I had had an abscess which had burst and done untold damage. I was very poorly and my weight was down to about six stone. As soon as I felt well enough, however, I went back to nursing; I was sure that this was my field of work.

About a year after we moved to Nottingham the trouble flared up again, then again about six months later. Then it kept on recurring. Sometimes, when I am better, some people say, 'I can't believe you have ever been ill.' I used to get a bit upset as I thought they didn't believe me. I now think it is a mark of God's hand. For me to be so ill and not to show it in my face or in my personality I think is a mercy.

When Matthew became a curate we thought about adoption. At the time I was commuting to Elstree studios to make a series of six films for mothers about having a baby. I decided then that I could not continue work and adopt a baby. I wanted to give myself wholeheartedly to being a full-time mother. So I stopped clinical work then. I haven't gone back to it since and I really miss it.

We had Angus from birth. He was born at 8.55, we had the phone call at 9.15 and went straight to the hospital. It was the same with Pippa. We really do feel that they are our children. They are fifteen and twelve now, and we are reaching the adolescent bit.

When I was twenty-five I had a hysterectomy, was still off work and was getting a bit bored. I saw a competition for nurses to write an essay. I entered it and won. A publisher then asked if I would write a nursing textbook, which I did, in my field of speciality – obstetrics and gynaecology.

When it was published friends told me I should write about my experience of God: there were so many books about being healed, I should write about not being healed. I prayed, 'Lord, is this your idea?' Within half an hour I had nine aspects which became chapters with a Bible verse for each one. It seemed amazing. I said, 'OK, Lord, I take your point.'

When it was written, I sent it to Dr Anne Townsend and asked, 'You have written books; what do I do?' She phoned me and said, 'It is extraordinary. I have just signed a contract with Kingsway that I will find someone who will write on this very subject.' It was God's hand all the way along.

My father died just before Angus arrived. He was full of fun, and part of my inheritance from him is a lovely sense of the lighter side of life. At times, though, that feels quenched. I sometimes feel that I am drowning in so much pain. When you feel terribly sick you do withdraw into yourself, so I am not always jovial. When I am more aware of the lighter side of life I am also aware of the serious side, so the two are together. I would hate to be known for only one and not the other.

A few months ago it felt too dangerous to try to

look ahead. It would have been easier if I could say, 'OK, I am going to die folks, and I will do the heroic bit and do it well,' but it was harder to face the possibility of staying here and having the questions unanswered and having no escape.

Jane was concerned lest readers might think of her as always bedridden. God has been allowing her speaking ministry to continue, in a variety of settings. At Trinity Theological College her programme time was doubled because the students wanted to hear more about the intimacy with God in the dark times. Her talk was described as 'moving, humorous, profound and lively all at once'.

I was feeling terrible when I was interviewed for *Songs of Praise*. A number of people said I was looking well, and I said that was because the morphine was working. I wanted to be very honest that sometimes I find it hard to understand why God doesn't indicate to us what he is doing and why he doesn't seem to answer our prayers; though I am sure he *does* know what he is doing. Many people wrote in response to the interview. They told me in their letters that at last they had found someone who would be honest and would admit that God sometimes doesn't answer our prayers, or at least not in the way we wanted. That I still trusted in him gave them hope. It gave them the feeling that maybe they could trust him even though he was not doing what they wanted him to.

We have to be careful as Christians if we say God is trustworthy – of course he is trustworthy – but if we imply that he will do whatever we say, that actually makes *us* into God. I think there are

people coming to Christ whose hopes are raised –
that's great – but if their hopes are raised in a God
who will do whatever they want, then that's not
right. That's not the God that I know.

*We shared a brief time of prayer, then there was a
train to catch. Travelling back, there was much to pon-
der. Remarkably, Jane had evoked not sadness or anxi-
ety, but rather an exhilaration of spirit.*

6

ENOCH ADEBOYE

NO COMPROMISE ON HOLINESS

Pastor Enoch Adeboye sits facing me across a large, oval pine table which is empty except for a telephone and a penholder. The Nigerian pastor is wearing a white suit which matches the fresh white walls of the new London offices of the Redeemed Christian Church of God. Royal blue drapes at the windows behind him add a splash of colour.

He looks cool and relaxed. Two nights before, he had delivered a rousing address to nearly 8,000 people at one of the Festival of Life meetings at the nearby London Arena in Docklands. He had begun to speak at 1.10 am, for it was an all-night meeting of prayer and preparation for revival: a night too for praise and worship and for miracles. He smiles as he recalls it. 'Any Christian who comes all night is really committed.'

The story of Enoch Adeboye's ministry begins in 1973. He was lecturing in the mathematics department at Lagos University when he was born again.

It was a problem that really brought me to Christ: a problem that all my mathematical equations couldn't solve. Someone invited me to the Redeemed Christian Church of God. He said, 'Come, miracles are happening here.' So I went, looking for a miracle. When I got there, they preached salvation to me. I resisted, because all I wanted were the miracles. I was willing to pay for them.

After a month the problem remained but I could see that there was something about these people that was beautiful. I could see the peace of God in them; the glory of God. I thought that even if I didn't get the miracle I came for, I wanted what these people had. So when they gave the altar call, I responded and of course that was the turning point. God gave me the miracle I had wanted and he gave more, much more. My ambition had been to become vice-chancellor of the university, but the Lord called me to ministry.

The Redeemed Christian Church of God began in Nigeria in 1952 from a prayer meeting of a dozen people. It spread throughout Nigeria and then, twelve years ago, began in Britain with just four people at the first service. Now there are thirty-nine churches around the country. New ones are starting in Germany and Holland.

In 1980, the founder of the Redeemed Christian Church of God had gone to glory and he had written in his will that I was to succeed him, so I became the General Overseer. Membership of the church has increased at such a rate that it's hard to keep up. It's somewhere between one million and two million. God will know the right figure. Last year we ordained over two thousand pastors, including thirty-one in London. We now have a Bible college in Zambia for Central Africa.

We judge the pastors not just by academic knowledge. Before someone can be recommended for ordination he must have pastored a church for a time and have proved that he has the ability. In the Pentecostal Church it is more important that the gifts of the Holy Spirit are in operation than how many degrees you have.

I was married before I became a Christian. My wife Folu was not a believer then either, but we came through to faith together. We have three sons here in Britain: one has just graduated from university, the other two are in high school. Our daughter has gained her degree in Nigeria. Praise God, they all love the Lord. I thank God for them; they are a wonderful blessing.

Folu often travels with me and she has fasted with me. When I decided that I was going to fast for sixty days, we had agreed at the beginning that by the time we reached the forty-day mark she was to stop. After forty days she said she would go all the way with me, but I was not sure that she could physically continue. So I had to break on the forty-second day. It is a miracle to have a wife who will agree to fast like that with you. We are very much of one vision, one purpose.

The all-night Festival of Life meetings at the London Arena are not simply black Pentecostal gatherings, though they were almost entirely so when they started. Many more white Christians are now coming, from across the denominational spectrum, and a variety of Christian leaders now take part. Pastor Adeboye explains how the central purpose is to affect the national spiritual climate, an essential element in revival.

You can't keep bringing thousands of people together to pray all night without something happening in the spiritual realm. You see, when the children of God get anointed and they pray more, it becomes easier for the almighty God to do what he wants to do in their particular country.

The Word of God is clear in 2 Chronicles 7:14, that 'if my people that are called by my name will humble themselves and pray . . .' His people have to do the praying. This verse says that if they will pray and turn from their wicked ways and seek the Lord, they will hear from him and he will heal their land. Sadly, holiness is often lacking today. It's a word that's not heard as often now in Christian circles as it once was. But we can't compromise on this at all. Holiness is really the foundation, the key in preparation for revival. Holiness simply means obedience to God. Without holiness, no person shall see God.

We have these events at night because there is plenty of time. In a crusade people can begin to get a bit fidgety because they want to go home. But at night there's time for in-depth teaching of the Word of God. When you get to a certain time of the night you no longer want to go home. You want to see it through to the end. Because of the intensity of all that is going on, you forget all about the time.

I like to bring in everything, because not only am I addressing committed Christians, I am calling on new believers and I am preaching to those who have come out of curiosity just to see what's going on. Many of these people get saved.

I believe that London has a big role in a coming revival in Europe. Before long I believe the arenas will be too small, then it will be on to the stadiums. The world will pay attention. There are plenty of dark clouds now. The devil senses that revival is coming and is having his fling. There is the rising crime and violence, the break-up of families, social problems. But God has his purpose and will not be thwarted. After dark clouds comes rain, not just showers but a real downpour.

In Nigeria, the monthly Holy Ghost Service (or the Festival of Life as the London version is called) has become the biggest regular event in national life, with crowds of up to 300,000 people from different churches and backgrounds. The vast crowds gather at a site mid-way between Lagos and Ibadan. There are also now local versions in other major towns. It all began in a small way in Pastor Adeboye's own church, as he explains.

Twelve years ago I was here in London and was spending time with the Lord a few days before my birthday. I was astonished when he asked me what I wanted for my birthday. I didn't know that God would be interested in anybody's birthday. After a while I pulled myself together and said, 'Lord, if that's what you are asking me, I want a miracle for every member of my congregation.' His reply was that I should call the members together and he would meet the request. That was how the Holy Ghost Service began.

I went back to Nigeria and invited every one of them, as many as would come, to a programme lasting a week. On the first day 600 people came and miracles started to happen. On the second day 2,000 came. When we came to the third day, Wednesday, in order to get a seat, people were already in church by 8 a.m., although the programme wasn't due to start until 6 p.m. It was a beautiful experience in the Lord. It was so glorious that people began to pray that the programme

would be repeated the following year. That went
on for six years. Then, in 1993, because of the numbers who were coming, we reduced the event to a
weekend programme.

Interest grew so much that we were then asked
to have the event every month. I knew what a
strain that would be for me, because of the preparation in prayer and fasting. But I knew it would
be very beneficial for the people. So we started the
Holy Ghost Service monthly in Lagos, an all-night
programme on the first Friday in the month, starting at 7 p.m. and finishing around 6 a.m. We chose
Friday because most people don't go to work on
Saturday; so they could spend the whole night in
prayer, hearing the Word, praising God and being
free in the Spirit.

The miracles kept multiplying and the crowds
kept coming. When the attendances grew to
100,000 we started to build a new auditorium with
twice the capacity.

That was in 1996 and it is now overflowing.
Each time well over 10,000 people are being saved.
The event became so big that it attracted government attention because of the traffic jams that were
occurring on the Lagos–Ibadan expressway. When
the Holy Ghost Service started I thought it was
something for my denomination. But, as it has
expanded, I find that this is for the body of Christ.
Many people from traditional churches come,
including bishops. There are also leading figures
from national life.

We find that sinners come seeking miracles and
at the end they give their lives to the Lord. Church
members who are already converted come because

they want to hear the Word. In the process they are touched by the Holy Spirit, their knowledge of the Word deepens, they go back to their various churches and now the level of spirituality, even for ordinary church members, has grown tremendously. If we are all involved together, nobody will see this as a ploy to draw sheep from one church to another. I want to avoid that at all costs, because this is meant to be a revival for the body of Christ. We have seen in Nigeria that, as the various churches have begun to come together, they have come alive, they have been touched.

If God wants to bring a mighty revival to Europe, as I believe he does, then the revival should not be put in a little corner, in one compartment. No, let's walk together, let there be revival for everyone and let the almighty God be the only one who takes the glory.

7

PATRICK DIXON

'I WAS TOLD TO GET READY FOR SOMETHING BIG'

Amid the rows of villas in Ealing in west London I found the Dixon residence with a workmen's hut outside and drilling going on. A mud-spattered plank led up to the front door. Part of the foundations had been found to be shaky. They were having to be underpinned and renewed. This is what Dr Patrick Dixon is helping to do, I thought, in the context of today's society.

Often in demand for radio and television interviews, he broadcasts from home, using virtual technology. I had heard about his virtual office and it was there that we headed upstairs. He scrolled through all the topics covered on his web-site. He is getting 700 visitors a day on the Internet – 'just imagine that in terms of correspondence' – requesting around 4,500 pieces of information: web tv, features, comment.

As we settled downstairs, Patrick did a quick calculation. He had to pick up a couple of people at Gatwick airport. From their time of arrival, he estimated time to clear the airport, the distance, speed of driving at that time of day, and his rate of speaking, at just over 5,000 words an hour. He reckoned the interview should finish at 3.10. It did.

What are the roots of the distinctive and exceptional

ministry to which God has called this servant?

I was brought up in Wimbledon in south London as an Anglican. My parents have a consistent Christian faith and took us to church. I have two younger brothers, both of whom are strong Christians. One is a Baptist minister in the East End of London and the other works in advertising.

As a child I was full of energy and very creative: always making things, building things and constantly writing. I have kept the many diaries I wrote, as well as a first novel written when I was eighteen; it was unpublished, but I now have a thriller being published by HarperCollins.

I have always believed in God, but it was through being confirmed as an eleven-year-old that I came to understand what it meant to have faith. I was confirmed by a really godly man. It was the point of commitment for me, in front of my family, my friends, everyone.

I went to King's College, Wimbledon and landed up reforming the Christian Union. At the same time, Sheila, who is now my wife, was doing a similar job in Wimbledon High School. We met at a Christian conference when we were fifteen or sixteen and have been best friends ever since.

My father was a civil servant so we were a reasonably well-off family, living in a large house. When I was in my late teens my father was seconded to the embassy in Washington for three years. I enjoyed this time and it stretched my horizons. I then went to South Africa for three months, to work at a mission hospital in the Transkei. This gave me a more global perspective.

I went to Cambridge to read medicine without any great sense of a call into that sphere. I tried to escape it in my second year and came back to London. I took a sabbatical year to run a computer company before going back to medicine.

I was always convinced, however, that I would end up in Christian service outside normal conventional career paths.

After qualifying, I worked at St Joseph's Hospice in east London, which was hard emotionally but deeply satisfying. I decided after a couple of years to work part-time with a community care team at University College Hospital, bidding farewell to a career path in medicine and giving the rest of my time to help lead a local church.

For several years I had a strong sense that change was coming; that I needed to get ready; that I would often be speaking publicly. During that time I made notes throughout my Bible, set up card indexes, studied and read and read. Today the demands on me keep coming thick and fast. With little time to prepare, I am drawing on the wealth of resources laid down in those early years.

In March 1987 I was asked, as a terminal-care doctor, to go onto an AIDS ward for the first time. I didn't want to do it. My attitude was rather harsh and judgmental. I felt this disease had come upon people because of the way they had behaved. When I went onto the ward, however, I was completely shaken, confronted by a ward full of gay men who were dying long before their time.

The first person I saw was dying in the most appalling circumstances – tubes in every orifice and suffocating alone in a glass cubicle. He was

obviously scared, without the basic support we
had learnt from the hospice movement – to help
people's breathing, their sense of well-being – and
his family wasn't there. I went back the following
week and he had died. But my advice had been
heeded, his family had been called and, given the
right medicines, he had died peacefully.

Here was a man, made in the image of God,
who needed help. Who was I to turn away? With
Dr Rob George I helped to set up a community
care team in London under the National Health
Service and began to get invitations to speak to
church leaders across Britain about this illness.
Wherever I went people were already challenged,
prompted by the same Holy Spirit. We needed to
have a compassionate, caring response, while
holding onto our Christian values and our beliefs
about God's design and purpose for living.

Someone from Kingsway Publishing was at one
of my first talks and asked me to write a book. This
was at the height of the government's AIDS campaign. There was very little Christian response at
that time, with notable exceptions including the
Mildmay Hospital. I was ready and six weeks later
The Truth About AIDS was finished and within
four weeks of it going to press it was in the shops.
It compared government statements with the real-
ities of the situation. I found a larger can of worms
the deeper I looked.

This book, like others I have written, had a ten-
point plan for the government and a ten-point
plan for the church. In the month before it came
out, people gathered round to pray. They realised
before I did what the impact would be. I had never

done a media interview before. I was completely naive.

The day the book came out it was front-page headlines in the *Evening Standard*. The front page of *Today* and the *Daily Express* also carried it – and their editorials called on the government's chief medical officer to resign. It was a strange situation; a completely unknown Christian writer, a part-time medic, working in a local church, writing his first book after seeing a couple of AIDS patients, and now facing television cameras and the rest of the media. Amid it all I was prayerfully asking, and discovering, what it was that we should do as a nation, as a church.

We started with nothing and trained fifty people in the YMCA at the end of the road. Several churches were involved. We began looking at ways of training people to go into homes as volunteers, to do what we could as a community-based organisation. We did it under the umbrella of Pioneer, as some of us were members of a Pioneer church, and Pioneer gave us a lot of encouragement – especially Gerald Coates. We didn't feel it was right to raise funds at that stage; but many people were telling us to get ready for it to become very big. Having seen what happened with the book, I took such comments far more seriously.

Three months after the book came out a very large Christian Trust, World in Need, offered the initial funding for ACET (AIDS Care Education and Training). It became one of the largest independent providers of community care for people with AIDS in the UK and started an educational programme in schools distributing over a million booklets and seeing 250,000 pupils face to face. It also developed work in ten other countries across the world.

The response to The Truth About AIDS *showed Patrick Dixon that a book could be a powerful catalyst for change.*

I was completely unknown, but became to some extent a national voice on the issue. Some 400 reports appeared in the national press over the following years, with hundreds of radio and television interviews. It's a responsibility to use that influence wisely.

If there hadn't been a book there wouldn't have been ACET. Now there's a global network of Christians working together in a common cause with unconditional love for all who are affected.

Kingsway suggested another book, *The Genetic Revolution*. It's a resource for the church and it has provoked national debate. I didn't have faith for it to sell more than a few thousand copies, but I was confident the message would reach millions, and it did. The *Mail on Sunday* ran a full-page exclusive, and that was just the start. Likewise, when *The Rising Price of Love* came out, there were half a dozen major articles in the national press, as well as television and radio coverage. Other books have ranged equally widely, from Parliament to cyber community. Now I am being asked to speak not just about the future of cloning, or cyber churches, or British politics, or AIDS, but the totality: 'What is your vision of life beyond the millennium?' That of course includes world revival – another book. They get the whole package. It's all about the

future global change. I have called my company
Global Change.

In June 1998 ACET celebrated its tenth anniversary at Lambeth Palace, with the Archbishop of
Canterbury and Sir Cliff Richard. I was involved in
leading it for three and a half years. I am best as a
motivator and communicator, but was trying to
run an international charity as a service to the
community. I was pleased to do it but even more
pleased to hand it over to Maurice Adams. Today,
as a patron, I am still very involved and have been
to India for ACET twice in the last year. But I am in
the right place again, which is to motivate and
encourage rather than to run.

Sheila and I had been part of the leadership of
Ealing Christian Fellowship for ten years. In 1991
we were asked to lead a church 'plant' in the inner
city. We said we would need a really good team –
I was still full-time with ACET – and Bridge
Church was born in Brentford. Now my role there
has been handed over as well, although we are
both still very involved.

* * * * *

A believer who is a very senior figure in one of the
world's largest banks rang me one day and asked
me to give a high-tech multi-media presentation to
bankers on global trends. It went well. Other presentations followed, and many organisations
began to tap in, including the World Economic
Forum and household-name multinational companies.

Key themes are the impact of the digital society,
virtual companies, widespread tele-working. Will

we still have relationships? What happens to family life? What happens to the soul of a community? What happens to values, meaning and motivation? These are fundamental issues for large and small corporations. They affect us all and strike at the root of our very being. What kind of world do we want to live in? We can clone sheep, perhaps humans tomorrow. We can take half a person's genes and put them into a monkey and they will work. We can take scorpion genes and put them into a cabbage.

Society doesn't know how to handle many of today's developments. We see them coming and there is a deep unease, a restlessness, as we come to the close of this millennium. This is a society where eight per cent of all international trade is illegal drugs: another 'sign of the times'. There is at the same time a global spiritual awakening. Western Europe, however, is a black hole spiritually: France, Portugal, Spain, Italy, Germany and to some extent Britain too.

I see a new church-planting movement into western Europe. If we don't release young Christians into this they will go anyway, without a sense of commissioning. When you look at the number of active, lively churches in Britain and then in France, for example, there is a huge gap. The work of such people as Charlie and Anita Cleverley in Paris has shown that the hunger is the same, though the culture may be different.

What we have done here in church planting in inner-city London, in Brentford, can be done just as well, though not without cost, in parts of Paris, Toulouse, Bonn or Frankfurt, and it needs to be done. If we don't do it then the Koreans will do it for us, or the Brazilians.

I believe that the wind of God's Spirit will blow ever more widely. It's going to happen.

Patrick Dixon's latest two books are *The Truth About Drugs* (Hodders, £6.99) and *Futurewise* (HarperCollins, hardback, £16.99).

His e-mail address is patrickdixon@globalchange.com and his web tv site is http://www.globalchange.com

The address of ACET is PO Box 3693, London SW15 2BQ (tel 0181 780 0400).

8

STEPHEN GAUKROGER
A LOVE FOR PREACHING AND THE WORD

The Chiltern Railways turbo whisked me from London's Marylebone into the heart of leafy Buckinghamshire, commuter-land with a semi-rural feel, in just twenty-three minutes. I was met at Gerrards Cross station and driven to nearby Chalfont St Peter – what an English image that name evokes – and Gold Hill Baptist Church, arguably the largest Baptist church in the land.

A minister's study can tell you a good deal about the person. Arriving early for my meeting with Stephen Gaukroger, I sat in his study taking in the scene. From floor to ceiling there were bookshelves lined mainly with hardbacks, first and foremost Bible commentaries arranged in Bible order from Genesis to Revelation. Here were the well-ordered resources of the scholar and teacher, student and preacher. The desk was remarkably uncluttered and the drawers of the filing cabinet each carried a label listing in alphabetical order the topics within.

Stephen arrived, unflustered in the midst of a busy day and looking as neat and tidy as his study. He is now in his fourth year at Gold Hill, after fourteen years in Luton. A speaker at Spring Harvest and Keswick, pro-

lific author, much in demand as a Bible expositor, president of the Baptist Union 1994–95, how did his journey of faith begin?

I was born in Sheffield, but the family moved to Preston when I was four and my sister Sue was just a year old. My parents were both committed Christians who lived out their faith. I owe them so much for the foundations they laid in my life.

When I was six or seven I asked to go to the adult evening service one Sunday. I can't remember the service but I clearly recall coming home, kneeling beside my bed and asking Jesus to come into my heart. It seemed a natural thing to do; no big deal. My spiritual growth has always seemed unremarkable; even the experiences of the Holy Spirit. It's been a touch of God here and there, a particular blessing at this point and that. It's been a process rather than a crisis, all along the way.

Pastor Fred Wilson in Preston was a significant influence. He gave me a part in leading services when I was only fourteen or fifteen and I preached my first sermon at sixteen. Meanwhile I had become chairman of the school Christian Union.

As a teenager I had a dream of a cricket career and it was a thrilling moment when I was told that I had been picked to play for the town team. The next moment I faced a painful decision. The match was to be played on Sunday afternoon – and I had promised to teach a Sunday-school class. Difficult though it was, I firmly made up my mind. I would keep my promise, even though it meant turning down this chance to step up from schoolboy cricket. They couldn't believe it, and I was not picked again. For me it was a defining moment. From then on my calling to Christian ministry became clearer and clearer.

After reading for a business studies degree in Manchester, Stephen trained for the Baptist ministry at Spurgeon's College, of which he was to become president in 1997. Annually a final-year student was selected to spend a year at the First Baptist church in Dallas. Stephen was chosen from his year. It was there that he met Janet.

I went to Dallas determined to stay single, but I found Janet's charms irresistible. She had just moved to Dallas, to study for a degree at the nursing college. As the church had 20,000 members it was something of a miracle that we met. I was working in the 'college and career' department and Janet was leading a Bible study.

On our first date, I said, 'I would like us to go out together and pray about it. If at the end of a year it feels right, I'll ask you to marry me.' Janet was stunned. 'I have never heard anything like it,' she said. She went back to her room-mate and said, 'Some strange Englishman has just said the wildest thing to me.' However, we became engaged. I returned to England for a year while Janet successfully completed her degree course, then I flew back for our wedding in Dallas.

Stephen became minister of Stopsley Baptist Church in Luton, where they remained for fourteen eventful years. The congregation more than quadrupled, to 400, in those years. Stephen was invited to become a speaker at Spring Harvest and became increasingly in demand as a speaker and writer.

His first book, It Makes Sense, *in 1986, was repeat-*

edly reprinted and translated into half a dozen European languages. It has been followed by another fourteen books.

Spurgeon's gave me a love for preaching and the Word. My aim is to take the Bible and bring it alive in a contemporary culture. I want to relate it to the 95 per cent of the time that we don't spend in church. If I have a regret it is that until recently I wasn't discerning enough in accepting or rejecting speaking opportunities. Sometimes I have travelled long distances and then felt they didn't really need me. I have prayed, 'Please, Lord, I don't want this to be simply a performance.' That may have been what was expected. I love working, but at last I have come to realise that I don't have to say yes to everybody's requests.

Speaking at Spring Harvest has helped me to get to know other Christian leaders. I have good contacts across the spectrum and enjoy the networking process. I keep an interest in cricket and like spending a relaxing day at Lord's. For exercise I enjoy playing tennis at the David Lloyd Centre at Heathrow, often very early in the morning before the day's work.

Gold Hill is blessed with a strong staff team. Stephen's predecessor, Jim Graham, is now director of external ministries; there is an associate minister, a youth minister, a church administrator and two secretaries.

The wider mission is not neglected; far from it, and support is expressed in practical ways. Next to the church is a mission house, used by mission workers on leave; the church contributes to forty-five of them and there are three cars for their use. There are mission prayer groups and a mission council. What are the financial implications of all this? How is the large budget raised?

This is a very committed community: warm, generous people. At our gift day we expect to raise £60,000. This would be regarded as an affluent area, but there are people here whose jobs are precarious and businesses threatened. There are the casualties: high earners who suddenly find themselves out of a job. This is a big church, with spiritual resources, but there are great needs all around us. We want to see the people of this area won for Christ.

Our conversation leads on from there to revival. How near does Stephen think it is?

There is a great expectancy in the air, but revival is a sovereign work of God. He could do it at any time. Real revival is measured in terms of large-scale conversions and social change, reaching out to the people who are begging, the homeless, those without hope. Massive tracts of the church are wholly untouched by such concerns. I want to see the gospel penetrating our education system and affecting the condition of the poor. There are huge differences in modern society. It can be said of many folk that 'their god is gold and their creed is greed'.

Stephen has weighed carefully what is being experienced in many churches – 'there are those who attribute nothing to the Holy Spirit and those who attribute everything to the Holy Spirit' – and he takes a well-considered and balanced view.

We have prayer ministry at the end of our services here. We have seen tears and other releases of strong emotion, including manifestations of the Spirit. It may be better for this to happen in this context rather than in the services. It is a threat to an individual's dignity and respect if it occurs in front of a large number of onlookers. There can be too much of a spectator mentality; of voyeurism.

Sometimes these days it seems that the carpet has replaced the altar as the place of spiritual devotion. But the carpet is the place of ease; the altar is the place of personal sacrifice. Seeking to grow in spiritual experience does not mean more falling over but deeper discipleship and obedience. Inadequate follow-up and lack of nurturing means that some Christians never really grow up. They are biblically illiterate and are prey to other influences. Lack of discipline leads to bad behaviour.

Stephen is concerned about family life today and the atmosphere in which children are growing up. He finds that his children talk of things he had not known about until he was sixteen. The topics are picked up in the playground. He candidly admits that one of his desires is to be a better husband and father.

We have three children: Bethany, who is fourteen, Cara, aged twelve, and Samuel, who is nine. I enjoy watching videos with the children: we have the same favourite cartoon characters. Janet likes strong drama, but when I have had a day of dealing with real-life problems I want something lighter for relaxation. I do enjoy reading biographies though.

Janet has a ministry of her own, taking seminars, leading worship, working with under-fives, giving evangelistic talks, but she is supportive of my ministry. Sometimes we do seminars jointly. We joke that's how we get to spend time together. For my own spiritual input I enjoy listening to tapes, especially some of the Spring Harvest addresses, and I find the elders here at Gold Hill a spiritual resource. They are very affirming.

9

PHIL WALL

FROM RIOT SQUAD OFFICER TO EVANGELIST

The Salvation Army headquarters in London's Queen Victoria Street is a spacious 1960s building which was opened by the Queen Mother. This information is picked out in gold lettering in the entrance lobby, alongside the list of International Commissioners. I ran my eye down the list as I sat waiting for Phil Wall. Officers would appear occasionally from the 'wings' or down the staircase ahead, in white shirts with Salvationist epaulettes, dark trousers and black shoes, moving about their administrative business.

This is not really Phil Wall's milieu. He is very much an out-and-about man at the roots; mission team leader based in Morden. He comes to headquarters once a week and then has to fit many appointments into the day, as he explained when he emerged for this interview. It began over a welcome cup of tea in a corner of the deserted canteen. He grinned when I asked him if he came from a Salvation Army family.

I am a foetal Salvationist – I was there before I was born! My parents were both Salvation Army officers from working-class backgrounds. They were gloriously saved. The Salvation Army gave them their future. God did the rest, and I am part of that story.

My father comes from the south coast and my mother from London's East End. Single Salvationists were brought together in those days and that is how my mum and dad met. I think it was at Sunbury Court, where we have many of our conferences. I am their only son but I have two sisters: the older one is a cadet at our training college and the other, who is married, is an opera singer and music teacher.

I was born in Hackney in east London and have moved about fifteen times in my life. We moved around a great deal when I was younger because of my parents' work as Salvation Army officers, including six difficult years in Belfast. But there is nowhere other than London that I would call home.

When I was sixteen years old I would do all the sorts of things teenagers do. I very much went my own way. It was at that age that I left home and joined the police cadets – something I had always wanted to do. I had made all sorts of silly mistakes and it was only when I was coming up to twenty that I really began to consider Christ seriously. I was challenged by some very gracious people who asked me if I believed what the Bible said about Jesus was true. Despite my years in church I had not given that a thought before.

I had made some sort of commitment as a young teenager but it was only at this stage that I realised that it was true that Christ died, and rose again from the dead. I wanted to have the new life that went with this truth. That was the time I did. There have been many ups and downs since then.

When I became a Christian there were several other Christians in the police station at Wembley where I worked and they were very supportive. I was a riot squad officer for about eighteen months and then for a couple of years a physical training and self-defence instructor. I had quite an easy ride in the police because of sport; I was a good boxer.

As a new Christian, however, I did not always make the right decisions. I had to face several lifestyle challenges, and changes to my aggressive attitude and responses to situations. The more mature Christians I worked with and knew, especially my youth group leader, David Hoyle, were a great help to me in those early days. I tended to be tense and aggressive about my faith, but I did see my brother-in-law, also a policeman, come to Christ during that time.

Phil Wall met his wife Wendy in Harrow, where they belonged to the same youth group and she was instrumental in Phil's conversion. They were married in Wendy's first year at the Central School of Speech and Drama, while Phil was still a police officer.

I was sharing my faith more and more; people asked me to tell their friends and I began to have preaching engagements. I felt called to leave the police to be more involved with my church and to work locally as a youth and community officer.

Wendy and I started out with no wage coming in, as such, yet we had a mortgage to meet. During those eighteen months God provided for us in miraculous ways. After that I went to Moorlands Bible College to get a diploma in mission. I had hoped to work with Youth for Christ, but Derek Copley, the college principal, encouraged me to work with the Salvation Army. I am now into my ninth year as mission team leader.

There are sixteen of us in all: full-time staff, volunteers, full-time trainees and a creative arts group. We go to Salvation Army corps and all sorts of other places as well, including universities. We are also involved in events like Spring Harvest. We reach out to people and we resource people, but we also have much to learn from others. For the first three years we were rushing about all over the place, but we prefer now to do longer-term missions. Wendy has travelled with me a great deal but that's not so possible now, with three children.

I am a driven person who finds it hard to relax. I play with our children, I run, I read a great deal and I enjoy being with friends. I love being with my wife and children and I know that if I am not good at that I am nothing. Credibility begins and ends at that point.

Phil is steeped in the Salvation Army, not only because of his family background but because of his love of all that is fundamental to it. He sees not only a renewal movement within it but a renaissance of all its dreams. There is a hunger for the early vision; for the passion, the militancy of its commitment to justice as well as evangelism, holiness as well as celebration.

If we want our life to count for God then we have to win our own battles for the heart, the mind and the will. I hear many Christians saying 'We want revival', but they can't even get on with the Christian brothers and sisters in their fellowship. There is a lot of rhetoric about militant, radical Christianity, but it's not about singing songs loudly, or jumping up and down, or even receiving a blessing. It's about the power of holiness enabling us to win these battles of the heart, mind and will. It has to be reflected in our lifestyles, our cheque books, our homes and families.

Phil is glad to work together on occasions with leaders from other streams. In particular he has worked with Gerald Coates, Steve Chalke, Sandy Millar and others of similar vision at the Roots event. This brings together several thousand people each year in ministry and worship and is as much a manifestation of God's Spirit as a hunger for more.

Phil is serving widely, even internationally, but also at a very local level.

Wendy and I and half a dozen others planted Raynes Park community church, the Salvation Army's local expression, where we live, near Wimbledon. This group of Christians from the area is trying to reach the community with the gospel. We meet in a school. The average age is about twenty-five, and at thirty-five I am the oldest leader. About 30 per cent of the members are historically Salvationists; 70 per cent are either converts or Christians from other churches who have moved into the area. Thankfully we have not had many transfers from the local churches.

What hope does Phil Wall have for the future?

I am very hopeful about the future. People are getting cynical about institutions and they are turning away from institutional Christianity. At the same time they are incredibly hungry spiritually. Increasingly they will look to those who will express an authentic spirituality that touches the real world and engages with its pain.

The Salvation Army is engaged in a 'sleeves

rolled up' kind of spirituality. It is one of the most influential Christian groups in the world. We have massive credibility in the eyes of the public. As Bishop Lesslie Newbigin challenged us, this needs to be invested as risk capital for the kingdom.

My dream is to see the Spirit creating red-hot Salvationists who are passionately in love with Jesus and will lay down their lives to see this world won for God.

10

TERRY VIRGO

'NO WELL-WORN PATHS AHEAD OF YOU'

When Terry Virgo gave up a career in the civil service in his early twenties to live by faith as a door-to-door evangelist he could not have imagined where it would lead. He is now working with 140 churches in the New Frontiers International network, as well as nearly 60 more in twelve nations overseas. He leads the Stoneleigh Bible weeks, now attracting over 20,000 people each year. The Brighton conferences draw 2,000 leaders from Europe and further afield. He has written many books, including studies based on Bible characters.

In Brighton and Hove is where it all began. Terry Virgo travels the world and for two years he led a New Frontiers church in America. But it is to his home town that he has always returned. We met in the modern offices created within a redundant church building amid Hove's Victorian villas. Here is the nerve centre of the New Frontiers International network, combined with a centre for local youth activities, while the Church of Christ the King is now in the heart of Brighton, a multi-storey three-storey building seating 1,200, converted from a former warehouse.

I asked Terry about his childhood in Hove and how he came to faith and to his dedication to serving the Lord.

My parents were not Christians, though they sent me to the nearest Sunday school. My sister Marion moved to London for a theatrical career and was led to the Lord by a Billy Graham crusade convert. Marion came home to Brighton one weekend and said, 'I'd like to tell you something.' It was the first time I had heard the gospel. I had never heard the expression 'born again' before. I had never heard anybody talking as she did then: that she knew a personal Saviour, that she knew she was converted, knew she was going to heaven, knew her sins were forgiven.

It all sounded amazing – presumptuous I thought. But that night I actually knelt and received Christ myself and was born again. I knew it had happened to me. My parents were really not very interested. But I had the privilege of leading them both to the Lord many years later, individually, at different times.

I went to All Souls, Langham Place, where Marion was worshipping in London, and went forward at John Stott's guest-service invitation, shook the great man's hand and publicly sealed what had already happened. John Stott recommended a church in Hove to me, but it involved two bus journeys.

On my way there one Sunday it poured with rain and I sheltered in a Baptist church near my home. This was Holland Road Baptist Church and it became my home church. It was a flourishing church with about 600 members. Ernest Rudman was the pastor, a wonderful godly man with a heart for world mission. The church had a major impact on my life and I was baptised there in 1958.

I then slid back for a couple of years. I was twenty-one when I came back to God. A very dramatic sermon at the church turned my life around. By then I was working as a civil servant in Westminster, where I got to know a radiant Christian. He had been filled with the Holy Spirit and this led to my going to his church a few weeks later. His pastor laid hands on me and I was filled with the Holy Spirit.

I began using all my spare time witnessing, preaching on the seafront, leading the young people from the Baptist church into evangelism. My own pastor told me to lay hands on the other young people in the church, having heard what had happened to me, and as a result most of the young people in that church became baptised in the Spirit. We went out on Sunday afternoons, witnessing and singing and preaching to the crowds on Brighton seafront. We started doing evangelism on the housing estates at the back of the town.

In 1963 I left work to concentrate on this door-to-door evangelism. I did this for two years. I was reading books by people such as Hudson Taylor, about God supplying every need. For me it was a foundation time of proving God. I never published a prayer letter but I would receive gifts through the post. I moved to the housing estate where I was doing this work, and I needed money only to pay the rent, get petrol for my motorbike and buy supplies of *Challenge* newspaper to distribute door to door.

I began to get preaching invitations here and there, but after the two years I went to London Bible College, from 1965 to 1968. During this time

I met Wendy, my wife, who was from Plymouth Brethren background and lived in Leicestershire. We got married and I was then invited by a group of Christians in Seaford, a few miles from Brighton, to become the first pastor of a church they were setting up on a new housing estate.

When Wendy and I moved there, the building was not even built. We were able to introduce spiritual gifts and the laying on of hands on people. It was a free evangelical church which was one of the first to become charismatic.

A member of a group meeting in a home in Haywards Heath said to me, 'I know people who would like to be filled with the Spirit, would you please come and speak to them.' I went to his home and it was packed. I visited them on alternate weeks and the group grew and grew. Then when one of the couples moved to Horsham, I went there too, and their home filled.

Eventually I was going to about ten groups meeting in homes all around Sussex. They became house churches which just grew and grew, and I visited them on a regular basis. I was travelling increasingly, but by this time my home church had a growing team of preachers which meant I could be away more often on a Sunday.

We started the Downs Bible Week at Plumpton racecourse, which ran for ten years. The first year we had 2,700 people and it drew more each year, up to the 5,000 capacity. It then grew to 10,000 spread over two weeks. We gave it a break for two years, then found the Stoneleigh agricultural showground in Warwickshire, a massive place, much better equipped for such an event and of course in the centre of the nation. This year, 1999, will be our ninth year there.

When Terry Virgo had first left work he had felt God telling him that he would eventually serve him in the Brighton area. Approached by a small group who were meeting in a schoolroom there, he felt he should make this his base. The group quickly grew and were offered the Clarendeon mission hall, a run-down building with dry rot, which they renovated.

Numbers swelled to 400; the church sub-divided and this repeated until there were five congregations around Brighton and Hove, each with a full-time pastor. They then all came together for Sunday morning worship in the Odeon cinema, which could then hold 1,200 people. Seeking their own meeting place, they discovered the former Comet warehouse which was converted to become the present Church of Christ the King.

On the wider scene a number of pastors, most of them Baptists, asked for Terry Virgo's help. Their churches had become charismatic but they were uncertain how to proceed.

I started getting involved until I was working with a growing number of churches in London. Then one of our pastors had a vision of a herd of elephants charging into jungle terrain, breaking it down and creating a new way through. He gave this prophecy: 'There are no well-worn paths ahead of you but together you can make a road. Many will benefit. Together you can accomplish more than you can apart.'

I gathered the pastors together and shared this prophecy. I said that it meant a philosophical change. We had to be an identifiable group of churches, although each would keep its own title.

So there are many different names, such as Kings Church and New Life Church, and each one has autonomy; the local pastors and leaders have the authority, but we work together.

Within a year we had taken a team of sixty to Cape Town, where I was beginning to be involved, and spent three weeks doing street evangelism. We built some houses in a black township. I spoke at pastors' conferences. We started training programmes, even church planting. One of our churches alone could not have done this, but all of us together could.

I believe that the New Frontiers movement has a clear calling: to restore the church, to make disciples, to train leaders, to plant churches and to reach nations. Those are our purposes, but within them are many local expressions of church life, a good deal of diversity. We do feel nevertheless that there are certain priorities, such as the place of the Holy Spirit in the local church. We place a strong emphasis on the grace of God, the centrality of Scripture and plurality of eldership.

We don't have women in eldership. We have women doing many things: baptising people, breaking bread, laying hands on the sick, prophesying, casting out evil spirits; but we feel we can't ignore Paul's words, 'I don't allow a woman to teach or have authority over a man' (1 Timothy 2.12). We enjoy fellowship with other streams who would differ from us on such issues. I have excellent friendships with Gerald Coates and Roger Forster. We want our churches to have fellowship with other churches. In Brighton we chair an evangelical ministers' fraternal and we have started a prayer walk.

Wendy is a gifted speaker and has written four books. We are careful to guard Monday as our day off. We enjoy walking on the Downs, getting out into the country, walking and talking. We both cycle a bit and I used to play squash but now play racquet-ball, a game for older people.

We have four sons and a daughter, ranging in age from twenty-eight to seventeen. I have always tried to space out my times away so that I am not leaving them for too long. The older ones are becoming scattered but they are all serving the Lord in a tremendous way. Anna, our daughter, moved to Cape Town, where she has married a zealous young evangelist in the church there.

Terry Virgo never talked about himself for long; each time I prompted him to do so his conversation soon turned back to the ministry in which he is immersed. He is a totally committed servant of the Lord – and the Lord has taken that dedication and has used Terry greatly in the building of his church, the training of leaders and the nurturing of many, many thousands of Christians around the world.

11

BRIDGET PLASS

PLASS AND MINUS: THE COST OF A MINISTRY

'It's you I'm calling, not Adrian,' I said to Bridget when she answered the phone, 'because it's you I want to come and interview.' My experience in getting to the Plass home was like one of the personal incidents that Adrian can relate so amusingly. I took a wrong turning and went several miles out of the way. Back on course, I was almost within sight of the road when I got tangled up in a one-way system, finally emerging further away and totally confused.

Eventually I found my bearings and reached the road and the house. The door was opened by a woman who said, 'They don't live here any more.' Did she know their new address? No, she didn't. What now? Fortunately she could tell me roughly where the house was and could describe it. It wasn't too far away but by now I was late and somewhat ruffled. However, I was quickly reassured by Bridget, who emerged from the house, smiling and welcoming me as I parked the car.

We were soon chatting in a relaxed way in their comfortable sitting room and I asked Bridget first about her childhood.

I was born and brought up in a Christian family home in Norwich and went to a Roman Catholic junior school. My mother had been brought up a non-conformist, so it was rather a mixed upbringing. But I gained a lot from my Catholic schooling. I value the sense of mystery I found there. I think it suited me because I was an imaginative and rather volatile child. I loved going into the chapel and just being there on my own. It was so pretty and so odd; strange and different.

I went to university just when the sixties were beginning to swing. I had never thought through my faith, or worked out any answers. I met lots of people who were wallowing in all sorts of philosophies and different ways of thinking. My beliefs weren't really anything.

I was at Bristol studying drama, history and English. I always wanted to go on the stage and had always wanted to go to theatre school, but my dad didn't think that was very suitable. The compromise was that I did drama as well as English and history at university. When I completed my degree I went to the Bristol Old Vic and that is where I met Adrian. It was a small theatre school and you got to know everybody.

I thought Adrian was very strange; he was so different from most of the people there. I had wanted to be there for so long, but once I got there I found it very difficult because it was all about oneself. It was about projecting yourself – fair enough – it was about what you looked like and what you were and it was about how you sold yourself and I couldn't handle that. Obviously it was about other things as well; it is a very good theatre school, and it has produced some amazing people. I think I was perhaps just a bit raw. I got depressed and felt quite lost, certainly in my faith.

When I met Adrian his faith was everything and he kept talking about it. He wanted to start a Christian Union, which went down very badly, but I found it intriguing that someone could be so sold out to something. I wrote to him at Christmas and said that I was very interested in what he was talking about. Really because of that, he returned for the new term, after deciding earlier that he would not go back because he was so lonely there. That is how our friendship started.

Adrian was a very evangelical Christian at that stage and I think he would say quite pedantic! He had not had any corners rubbed off his faith then. It had solved a lot of problems for him when he was sixteen and he wasn't going to allow anything to change that for him. Such a faith offered me a lot of security; it was a very definite package. I went off to a little chapel and found it extremely embarrassing as I burst into tears in front of a lot of people I didn't know. I couldn't stop crying.

I can say that Adrian drew me to faith, but I am sure my parents did as well. They laid the foundation, but I got very confused in my teens. I saw God as someone not very nice, always very demanding of me and at times I got depressed. People think that I must be like Ann in Adrian's books; a very calm and balanced person. But I always say that Ann is Adrian's ideal woman. She is certainly not me. We have both always been 'up and down' sort of people: that's the way we are.

We remember being firmly led by God to leave the theatre school and go into social work. I had finished my course but Adrian had only complet-

ed his first year. We got a job together working
with very disturbed children. It was in
Gloucestershire at a place called Cam House, run
by committed Christians. We were the old-fashioned house parents and we both found it satisfying but very demanding. I have a natural love of
working with children and that is still where my
heart is. I would still love to be in social work. I
work on a voluntary basis now with children on
our local council estate.

Although Adrian had greater skills than I had,
he had no formal qualifications. So we decided
that he would go to teacher training college. That
was a way on in social work at that time.

*Adrian went to the college, Bridget took up a teach-
ing post to support them – and then they had Matthew.
A series of jobs followed, which led to Adrian running a
secure unit in Hailsham for teenagers who had 'got to
the end of the line'.*

It was very hard and demanding. The maxim is,
'you do not get involved' and for some people that
works very well. But you also need the people
with the really deep perception – who often end
up not being able to cope. This happened in
Adrian's case and was one of the reasons why he
cracked up. It was not the only reason, but it was
one of the strands in the whole situation. It was a
horrible time and I think it was a very difficult
phase for many people. It coincided with the time
when in many churches the teaching was that
healing was for all – and that if you were not
healed, there were reasons.

The concept of a breakdown was a tricky one. It
was the time of the big John Wimber wave which

brought so many good things into the church, but it did bring some silliness as well, which I don't think John Wimber would have condoned.

For seven years we had been doing an epilogue series for TVS called *Company*. It was a kitchen setting, with a group of people talking round a table. At its best it was really good and at its worst it was trite. We would go and record seven programmes in a morning. We had sifted ideas the night before, but it was fairly spontaneous. When Adrian became ill he continued to do some of the programmes. It was a difficult situation but the others taking part were very supportive.

Someone from Marshall Pickering saw the programmes and asked Adrian if he would write *Join the Company*. That was the first book before *The Sacred Diary*, which had begun as a column in *Christian Family*. It then became *The Growing Up Pains*, as what poured out when he started writing it was his own story.

Often when people go into ministry, they feel God calling them, they pray about it, they have confirmation about it – that's the normal way – but for us it was a complete muddle, a disaster even, as far as we were concerned. Then this little winding pathway appeared and we followed it, as it was really the only way to go. When *The Sacred Diary* was published, it just took off. We had not known or even expected it to happen. I just wanted things to be back to normal.

During the time when Adrian was ill I had prayed frantically for him. But again and again I had felt God say, 'But have you counted the cost?' I was very bewildered by this. I think God was trying to say to me, 'You are praying for his healing but you don't actually know what that is going to involve.' I just wanted him better. When we pray for healing for someone, or for a solution in their lives, we want everything to return to how it was before. The idea that everything is going to change quite quickly into something new would be awfully scary to contemplate.

There has been a great cost, as I think there is for families, as well as a great blessing. We have been through various stages. First it was wonderful; we were just so excited that God had got a job for Adrian to do. Then I found that I was having to struggle with all sorts of things in me that I hadn't faced. I think you put yourself on hold when you are coping with someone else's illness. I found that I was actually in rather a poor state and felt quite angry that God had got Adrian better just to take him away.

I am sure it was a spiritual attack as well. The devil attacks the weakest element, which I was at that stage. He kept wearing away to try and break the chain and prevent Adrian from doing what he was doing. I wanted Adrian to do good things for God, I wanted people to be set free by God; that was all very exciting. But there was confusion in me; God seemed to care so little that I had gone through so much, only for him then to whisk Adrian away as soon as he was better.

We began to talk about it as a job that God had given Adrian to do and I went away for a weekend retreat at Scargill House to try to sort myself out – I have written about it in my book *The Apple of His Eye*. All I could think about while I was there was

Jesus. Then on the way home I was caught in a severe snow storm on the M1. I ended up with my car broken down in the darkness in a side road in the snow, apparently miles away from anybody. In total despair I said to God, 'Now you have just done it again. I have been away on a lovely weekend, I really believed you were near me and here I am in the darkness; you don't care'.

I opened my eyes and there in front of me I could see a Travelodge and a Little Chef: a miracle especially for me. It was all so wonderful. I had somewhere to stay for the night, and I felt so much the humour and the love of God, and that he was there for me. I think these situations can often be quite silly – but when they happen to you, they matter to you.

That was really a turning point. I could start not minding about things, not worrying that Adrian seemed to be talking so much about us and giving away so much; to realise that was our job. People do ask, 'How do you cope when Adrian tells people everything about you?' But of course he doesn't. It's like the iceberg, he only talks about the bit above the surface. He doesn't talk about the rest because that is private to the family – but perhaps he still talks about a third more than other people do!

We have been having a sabbatical year. Adrian has been doing no speaking at all, and we have been getting used to having each other around for much more of the time.

Adrian loomed in the doorway, his large frame looking even bigger at home than on stage, to greet me before I left. He and Bridget were both obviously enjoying their sabbatical together. Adrian was nevertheless

*about to go on a journey next day to visit Matthew, the
eldest of their four children, who was teaching English
– in Azerbaijan.*

12

ROB FROST

DETERMINED TO BE AN EVANGELIST

The traffic was swirling along Worple Road on the one-way system opposite Raynes Park station on its way to Wimbledon. On a corner stood a large Methodist church and I spotted an open door. Inside, however, I found a pop-in café for pensioners, who were relaxing together over mid-morning coffee.

Along the side of the building, in the quieter Tolverne Road, I found the entrance I wanted and was greeted inside by a rather peaky Rob Frost. It was his day off and he had a heavy cold. But he was pleased to welcome me and to escort me through the offices. There were plain rooms with well-worn desks, basic equipment, and packages of literature and other paraphernalia of the various activities; a workaday setting with no frills.

Rob is at the heart of a remarkable range of activities; not only that, but in 1996 he gained his doctorate from King's College, London, after four years' study and research for a thesis on church planting and church growth, with radical conclusions.

He led me to an upstairs room for us to talk about his life and ministry.

I was born in Yorkshire. My father was, and still is, a Methodist minister and we lived in a village called Sowerby Bridge in a rambling manse.

When I was three years old my father was appointed minister of Swanbank Mission in the Potteries. I still feel an attachment to that church and have gone back and preached there several times. We hold many of our Easter People preliminary meetings there. The banisters that I used to slide down when I was six are still there. So are some of my Sunday school teachers. I was dragged to Sunday school three times every Sunday.

We then moved to Plymouth. As a young teenager, I was pretty rebellious, even in church. There was a girl who sat in front of me who had a long ponytail which I tied to the chair-back during a very long talk. Fed up with the whole thing, I eventually just rode my bike round a park on Sunday mornings. My parents were sad and upset about it.

When my father moved to a church in Birmingham I was drawn to a group run in Corporation Street on Sunday mornings by an unconventional character named Arthur Eden. There were no hymns or prayers or Bible readings. He would come in with two shopping bags and would take cups out of one and a jar of coffee and chocolate biscuits out of the other. He would sit back and say, 'What kind of week have you had?' He organised trips for the group and took us away to camp. Within eighteen months it had become a Bible study and prayer group and I really don't know how he did it.

At Easter we went to a Methodist mission

campsite at Alvechurch. I remember lying on my back and looking into the starry night and thinking, I wonder if there is a God, I wonder if all this is for real? That night I prayed something like this, 'Lord, I can't understand it all and accept it all, but if you are real be real to me'. That was the first turning point. My search had begun.

A year later, having read the Bible and argued with various people about the truth of Jesus' miracles, I finally gave in. I returned to the place where I prayed the first prayer and gave my heart to Jesus. It was wholehearted surrender. I asked him to do with me what he would. I received him as my Saviour, Lord and Friend. It was the end of a struggle and the beginning of a new peace.

The move from Plymouth to Birmingham dislocated Rob's preparation for GCE. His new school followed a different syllabus and Rob felt lost. He took nine O levels and failed them all.

I was devastated. My school sent me to the youth employment office, where I was asked to do peculiar games and puzzles. At the end of a solemn hour-long interview the man went away and came back with a card. He said, 'Well, Robert, we have evaluated your potential skills, and we feel that the only thing you are really suited for is the Army Pay Corps.'

I went home and there was a phone call from the head of a further education college at Bournville. I don't know whether he was prompted by someone else to contact me. Anyway, he asked me to go and see him. He was a gracious Christian man and he said, 'Give me two years of your life and I will demonstrate that you are not the failure you feel.'

At the end of the first year Rob gained seven O-level passes and after the second year secured two at A-level. He wanted to be a television producer so began studying film and photography and was all set for a three-year course in television production. Another Easter at the Alvechurch camp, however, when he was nineteen, led to a fundamental change. He felt he should give himself for full-time Christian service and went to Cliff College to train.

We did missions in various places. The first I went on was to a part of Sheffield. I witnessed to a biker in a fish and chip shop and he and his mates came to an evangelistic meeting. One of those lads went forward at an appeal and we counselled him and prayed with him. He was eighteen or nineteen and that night was killed in a road accident. Since then I have always felt the urgency of evangelism.

It took me four years at the Methodist college in Manchester to gain a degree in theology, years which I found immensely difficult. My first ministerial appointment was to a village near Barnsley. I then spent five years in Pontefract and three in Mitcham in south-west London. For two years while I was at Mitcham I was given half a page each week in the local paper to answer readers' queries. This led to a telephone helpline which was used by hundreds of people and was a forerunner of the Premier Radio Lifeline. I now have my own regular Sunday morning programme on Premier.

I have written four novels. The third, *Burning Questions*, is about an agony aunt and led to several meetings with the late Marjorie Proops, who asked deep questions about life and death over our meals together.

It was while he was at theological college that Rob first met Jacqui, who was to become his wife. He went to interview a church youth group for BBC Radio Manchester. Jacqui was producing a play about the prodigal son. A year later they met again at a mission and began to go out together soon afterwards.

We come from such different backgrounds: I come from the manse, her parents are from the casino and nightclub scene in Manchester. Jacqui was led to Christ by Ruth, the daughter of a children's evangelist. She and Ruth travelled to school together and Jacqui joined the Anglican church where Ruth went. Jacqui and I married, and Ruth married Paul Field, who is now responsible for the musical side of our drama presentations.

We have two sons, Andrew, nineteen, and Christopher, sixteen. Jacqui now works full-time in Christian ministry in the arts. Sometimes we work together, particularly at the Easter People event, sometimes independently. We both work very hard and then have frequent breaks. Jacqui paints and I love to write, particularly novels; that's the way I unwind.

For ten years Rob waged a campaign with the Methodist authorities for them to appoint him as an evangelist. Continually frustrated, he was about to go off and to work for Youth for Christ. Finally, however, it was agreed that he could become Methodist national evangelist, although there could be no house, no salary and no car with the job. He could, however, keep the title 'Reverend'.

That was in 1983. I prayed about it and it felt so

right. Fifty of our friends stood with us. A trust
came up with a salary and a retired minister's
house was found for us to live in. That was how it
started – on a shoestring. It's been an adventure
ever since, and still on a shoestring.

I remember the day that I gave my life wholeheartedly to the Lord and that is the foundation for
my whole ministry. For fifteen years I have had a
prayer partner, Clive Jones, a member of a charismatic church in New Malden. He has been a great
support to me spiritually over the years. I struggle
a lot with prayer. I think many evangelical
Christians pretend they don't and project a kind of
ease about it. I have found that it helps to pray
while out walking.

I am committed to drama and music in evangelism. The musical for the millennium, *Hopes and
Dreams*, is the culmination of two years' work. It
will be an opportunity for local churches to input
God's love into the community and for people to
come and share the church's millennium celebra-
tions.

We need to provide non-religious cultures for
people to come into church and discover worship.
I am helping to found a café-church based around
cappuccino and carrot cake on a Sunday evening,
with quiet jazz music and some Bible study and
discussion to try to create a non-religious environment in which people can relate to each other and
discover God and worship.

In a broken society the church has an opportunity to provide a strong community for belonging
and fellowship. I am committed to seeking revival.
It may not be the restitution of the church as we

knew it but a new spiritual wave of hunger for God.

The initiatives of the Rob Frost team include Share Jesus missions, Seed Team programmes for young people who give a year's service, the Easter People holiday week, and drama and musical tours. The latest production, _Hopes and Dreams_, has been playing to large audiences around the country and over 900 groups have registered to stage it themselves in the millennium year. For details of these activities call 0181 944 5678.

13

LYNDON BOWRING
THE LORD HONOURED, THE DEVIL RATTLED

When I first saw what appeared to be a block of tall townhouses in Romney Street, Westminster, I wondered if I had come to the right place. On the front door of number 53, however, was a brass plate with the word 'CARE' rather faintly etched on it. It is an appropriate location for an organisation concerned with moral and spiritual issues at the heart of national life. It is only some 400 yards from Parliament, where much of CARE's attention is focused.

At a practical level CARE co-ordinates various initiatives nationwide. Lyndon Bowring is its executive chairman; his right-hand man is Charlie Colchester, executive director. I announced myself on the Entryphone and was ushered up flights of stairs – there was no lift – to Lyndon Bowring's office on the top floor.

A passionate public speaker, Lyndon is committed to the cause with determination and tenacity. These qualities are matched with a warmth of personality and, above all, a love for people; people of all sorts and conditions. His roots are in South Wales, in the town of Caerphilly, famous for its cheese and one of Europe's largest castles. He appreciates his upbringing there.

My father was a very strong socialist in our town; they called him 'Red' Bowring. My mother was a lapsed Salvationist but came to a fresh faith through the ministry of Gladys Aylward. My father was subsequently converted through old-fashioned open-air preaching on the council estate where we lived. This happened to my parents when I was about ten years old and my brothers were thirteen and twelve.

It was awesome because we had come from a non-churchgoing, ordinary non-Christian family. We moved into turbo, because we then started going to church at least two or three evenings a week as well as on Sundays.

The local Pentecostal church we joined was vibrant, with a Sunday school of about 130 children and many teaching staff. The church was very active in evangelism and it became our whole social life as well. We met a lot of new people. I thought the church was wonderful, with many children of my own age; there were fifty or sixty of us in the youth group. In my late teens, however, I had a year in the wilderness. I never wilfully rebelled against the church, but I was living a double life.

The local grammar school was a great experience. I loved my school years; they were very happy. I didn't do much work but I seemed to do well. On the A-level course I was second in the English group to a boy who won a scholarship to Cambridge, but halfway through I left school and went to work in a fashionable department store. I don't know what seized me but I had a passion for fashion display and window dressing. From there

I went to work for the Inland Revenue – quite a contrast.

From the age of twenty I felt that God had called me. I had come across the Navigators and they transformed my life through the emphasis on Scripture memory, daily quiet times and so on. I wanted to invest my life in making disciples. I was helping to run a youth camp in Devon when I went out late one night to pray. It was then that I had an overwhelming sense that I should go to Bible college.

So in 1969, at the age of 21, I went to study at London Bible College. It was wonderful: a whole new experience for me, coming to London and meeting people from different denominations. It enlarged my Christian world-view.

I had done a lot of open-air preaching back in Wales. At Bible college I was the only student who volunteered to go and preach in the market square on a Saturday afternoon. It seemed a natural thing to do. In my preaching class at college I had to address fellow students. Gilbert Kirby, the principal, was our tutor. I finished my favourite sermon. 'Very good,' he said. 'Pity there was so much language of Zion in it, but apart from that it was good.' That was what I had grown up with: the Celtic language of Zion and revivalists. The college rid me of a lot of that and focused me, I was student director of evangelism for a year, and I loved that. I had relationships there that are still cherished.

To gain experience as part of their training, students in their second year were seconded to work with local churches. Lyndon, as Elim Pentecostal, went to

Kensington Temple. He soon got involved and was then asked to become assistant to the pastor, Eldin Corsie, which he was able to do in his third year. As his time at college came to an end he was invited to stay on at Kensington Temple, full-time.

It was a outstanding opportunity in an extraordinary church, with fifty nationalities and students from university colleges and medical schools. Eldin Corsie split the preaching and said, 'You do half and I'll do half.' He mentored me and discipled me and I am eternally indebted to him. Part of my brief as associate minister was to look after the fifty or sixty students there – there are now hundreds – on a Sunday evening.

It was because I had so recently been a student and was good at talking to people one-to-one, that I met a lovely young student who was president of the Christian Union at her teacher training college. She asked me to speak at her college. I thought she was the nicest girl around . . . We married and now have three children, two teenagers and a boy of nine. They bring us a lot of joy and a lot of fun. Celia is a great mum and wife and partner. She and I take parenting seriously and we jealously guard our time at home.

In October 1997 Lyndon was attending a CARE strategy meeting in London and Celia had gone to see her GP. After examining her, the doctor was concerned and sent Celia immediately to Charing Cross Hospital.

The time since then has been the most trying of our lives. We have cried more, prayed more, laughed more. The diagnosis is that Celia has multiple sclerosis (MS). It is different in every case. One of the greatest challenges with this disability is that you never know what tomorrow will bring. You therefore have to live a day at a time. Some days Celia is well and other days she is quite debilitated. But she is remarkable. She won't let this get the better of her. She has taught me so much and I think it has brought us closer together as a family. We did not realise how loved we were until Celia went through this: we have received so many letters and phone calls, some from people we have never met.

We live near the Thames in Chiswick and we love walking by the river. We go to our local health-club gym or to the jacuzzi, or we go swimming together. We love sitting and talking and finding a pleasant place just to enjoy companionship. We still worship at Kensington Temple. We are there most Sundays with our family. I am associate pastor, with Colin Dye the senior minister, and I sometimes preach. Colin describes me as being 'on loan to CARE'.

Lyndon's commitments beyond Kensington Temple grew. He chaired the working group of the International Year of the Child in 1978, putting on a big presentation at All Souls, Langham Place. He went on to chair the Nationwide Festival of Light, succeeding Eddy Stride, a great friend and mentor. He also became London director of evangelism for Elim churches. He realised that these responsibilities were becoming too big for him to continue his ministerial role at Kensington Temple. The Festival of Light kept expanding, to become CARE.

Lyndon is encouraged by the growing willingness of Christians to work together, to pray regularly and to campaign on issues of great concern. But he believes there is still a long way to go.

We have lost many battles; we have seen laws repealed, and new legislation introduced, that should not have been. A member of the House of Lords once said to me, 'While Christians were asleep in the 1960s lights went out in this House that may never be relit.' He was referring of course to the catalogue of laws that were passed often without Christians even knowing. They were not aware to pray, to fast, or do anything.

I long for more Christians to be involved in public life. I would love to see more Christian MPs, more Christian counsellors, more Christians working in the media. Every church should be praying regularly for the local radio, TV and press and for Christians to see the opportunities open to them.

I would like to see our society change to be more compassionate towards the marginalised, the poor; the elderly being made to feel cherished and special. I would like to see an end to issues being seen as 'right wing' or 'left wing', but rather in terms of right and wrong, issues to do with homelessness, refugees, the elderly, the unborn child, human sexuality, marriage, the family, care for the handicapped – right across the board.

One of the biggest encouragements for me is the depth of fellowship I have with so many leaders in London and in the wider network. There is a greater willingness among leaders to be honest and real, open and sacrificial, in terms of friendship. Celia is committed to helping ministry wives throughout the country through Living with Leadership; encouraging them and seeing their love and friendship develop.

We are seeing the importance of true friendship in Christ. It's happening and I think the Lord is honoured and the devil is rattled. I get a great kick out of that.

For further information on the work of CARE, and to support, call 0171 233 0455.

14

GERALD COATES

A PIONEER RATHER THAN A SETTLER

'I will give you your own teaching, training, prayer and revival centre. I see through its windows a beautiful, expansive garden and everything speaks of excellence: the long drive, the beautiful rooms. All sorts of networks will meet here: business people, young revivalists, musicians, people in authority. Prayer and revival will be its focus.' It was years after that prophecy was given – by an American, Dale Gentry, to what was then Cobham Christian Fellowship – before Gerald Coates was astonished by its fulfilment. It was in that very place, Waverley Abbey House near Farnham, Surrey, that I met him and his story unfolded.

My parents lived in Stoke d'Abernon, near Cobham in Surrey, and I have never moved far from there. I was their first child and I have a younger sister and brother. It was a decent home. My parents were nominal Christians and would go to church once or twice a year. They had a certain respect for the church, so we were encouraged to go to Sunday school.

My mother worked hard day and night to provide for us. My father had a very average job in plastics, although he became a designer and actually designed the first Perspex telephone booths which were attached to walls. But I think he was exploited; I don't think he ever got any money for it.

My years with my sister and brother were very happy. We lived in a council house in D'Abernon Drive, a road which also contained rather prestigious private houses. The builders had run out of money and council houses were then built. They were superior council houses, with central heating even in those days, but they were still obviously council houses.

The Sunday school I attended was at the Anglican church, St Mary's, Stoke D'Abernon. It was a very well-heeled congregation, but there were clearly people there who knew and loved the Lord Jesus Christ. My teachers were among them and, although they never knew it, they were influential in my life.

When I was eleven I was invited by my cousin to a youth camp in Salisbury. The idea of going away from my parents for two weeks at that age was appealing. I remember setting off in a brown lorry and then getting the train at Woking. The camp was run by a small organisation called the Latymer Youth Movement. The main sport was archery and it later became known as the Christian Archery Movement. It was run by a Mr Jeffreys, who attended the Gospel Hall in Cobham.

The first week was a nightmare. There were violent storms, tents were down, there was mud everywhere, meals were disorganised and it was chaotic. I cried a lot and was homesick. Then in the second week the sun shone, everything dried out and we got on with the fun of camping. In the evenings there would be a special visitor. We had somebody from MI5, an adjutant and a submarine commander, people who to a small boy had lived very intriguing lives and who told us how they had come to Christ.

One night I went back to my tent feeling that my life was not right without God. At the age of eleven I wasn't aware of sin at all in my life, it was a concept that was completely unfamiliar to me. It was very different in the next few years, but at that age I just knew that if God loved me this much, that he sent his Son to live for me and die for me and offer me resurrection life, eternity, then he was worth the rest of my life.

That was a most important day for me. At camp I was told, 'Now you've got to tell your parents you've become a follower of Christ. The longer you leave it the harder it will be.' When I told them they obviously had no clue as to what I was talking about. For the first time I felt alone, yet at only eleven I knew that something significant had taken place.

For some years I went each week to a little club run in Mr Jeffreys' house just round the corner from the school. We would have games and he would give us a Bible story and coffee. On Saturdays there would be archery. During the summer we would go off and do all sorts of things and they were very happy times. I was glad to be able to go to the home of someone who was a Christian and to discuss many questions.

You discover a lot about yourself between the

ages of eleven and eighteen, most of which I didn't like. There was a darker side. There were fantasies, just boyish things perhaps, but they became pretty mind-controlling. I found myself living a complex life: I was the most stable one of the three at home, a quite popular boy at school, where I became vice-head boy, a respectable Christian within the youth movement – there every Friday, every Saturday – but then there was another, secretive side, of immorality and dishonesty, this private fantasy world.

On a summer's evening in 1962, when I was seventeen, two of my friends walked round D'Abernon Drive, stood by a motor-cycle, and said, 'Is that yours?' I don't remember what I said but in a moment I was on this bike. It belonged to my sister's boyfriend and I was not insured to ride it. They pushed me down the road and I was away. I can still feel the breeze on my face; in those days there was no law about crash helmets. I felt pleased with myself as I began weaving between the parked cars staggered along the sides of the road where it narrowed. The last thing I remember is glancing over my shoulder – and at that moment the bike had a puncture. It went out of control, struck the kerb and I went straight over the handlebars, hit one of two brick pillars holding up wrought-iron gates, blinded my left eye, split my skull, and broke most of my bones.

I was rushed to Atkinson Morley Hospital. My parents were summoned but went home at midnight after being told that I could not survive the night. They went away thinking they had lost their eldest son.

I was unconscious for a week. I had left school
and was working in advertising and display in
Epsom and, when I eventually gained semi-con-
sciousness, my boss, Derek Horwood, and his
assistant were with my mother round my bed. I
didn't know what was going on. Through the
prayers of the Gospel Hall, which I had visited
once or twice with Mr Jeffreys, and the prayers of
people at work – many of whom were not
Christians but they prayed – I made a most
remarkable recovery after being given only four
hours to live. Three months later I was cooking for
a hundred boys at camp in Salisbury. It was a miracle.

I realised that when I was eleven God had
touched my life. I was now seventeen, living a life
of double standards, and the gap was growing
between what people thought of me and what I
actually was. At the age of eighteen I repented,
committed my whole life to Christ and joined the
Gospel Hall, which was the only evangelical
church in that small town. I was there for six
happy years. It gave me a very high view of
Scripture, a simple approach to worship, and good
friendships.

I was enjoying my job in Epsom and it was
there that I met Anona, who was to be my wife.
She wasn't a Christian when we first met. Our first
date was *The Sound of Music* in London. The next,
and the next, and the next, was an evangelistic
campaign in Cobham run by a Plymouth Brethren
evangelist named Jim Smith. Anona gave her life
to Christ during that campaign. She then came
with me to the Plymouth Brethren, the Gospel

Hall. I had been there for five or six years when I began to feel that, well, if we are so right and we are so biblical, and everybody else is in so much error, why isn't there more happening in our church?

We did a series of Bible studies on 1 Corinthians, in typical Brethren style, word by word, verse by verse. When we reached 1 Corinthians 14, however, about body ministry and tongues and prophecy, it was quickly dispensed with. I had never met a Pentecostal, had never heard of the charismatic movement, but I asked the leader, 'Sir, why don't we speak in tongues today?' – a purely academic question. Suddenly at the back there was movement and shouting: 'These young people, they're never satisfied with what they've got.' I was puzzled. To me it was such an ordinary question. I sadly wondered what I was on to here. Why wouldn't folk talk to me?

I worked out that if it was the work of the Holy Spirit to draw us near to Jesus, to magnify his name, then what I needed was more of the Holy Spirit. But how did you get more of the Holy Spirit? Did you go to more meetings or read the Bible more? For months I read anything I could on the Holy Spirit. Michael Harper's Fountain Trust meetings were a big resource for us – me and my wife and three friends. Denis Bennett from Seattle would be there, and Dennis Clark, Campbell McAlpine and Arthur Wallis. They became heroes to us. Those meetings and the few available magazines helped us understand that we weren't mad and we weren't becoming a sect.

After a while the leaders of the Gospel Hall

came to us and said they couldn't handle this. My wife and I and our three friends were faced with dissociation from the only group of people we knew who were born again, loved the Lord Jesus and had a high view of Scripture but who were totally anti-Pentecostal, anti-charismatic. They decided that they were not going to have any of this, so we were advised to leave: 'It would be better if you found fellowship elsewhere, Gerald.' It is actually a little more complicated than that because there was a split among the leaders and things going on in the church about which we knew nothing at the time.

We would like to have gone to Commercial Road Baptist Church, where David Pawson was minister, or to one of several other churches some miles away. The obstacle was that we had no transport. So we had to meet in our home. Anona and I had a tiny terraced house with no carpeting, no central heating and no telephone, a common situation for newly-weds at that time. It was a simple cottage meeting. We ate and drank together and there was worship, prayer, care for each other. This then drew other disillusioned believers to us and there were also a few conversions.

I don't think we ever set out to start a church. It was all very informal. We took up offerings and one day I went to the bank to open an account for the money. In what name? We had not thought about that. So I decided there and then on Cobham Christian Fellowship and that's what it was called for years afterwards before becoming Pioneer People.

We were still meeting in our little house – 41

Tartar Road, which is still owned by Christians today – and there would be thirty-five people crammed in the living room, in the hallway and up the stairs, worshipping and praying. The church at large was dismissive of us. Then, as we grew bigger, we were seen as a threat, so people spoke against us, though never to our faces. This went on year after year as the house church movement, now called by sociologists the new church movement, grew and spread. Our own meetings moved from our home to a local Girl Guides hall. When numbers reached 150 we had to move again, to a local school hall, where growth continued, to 250–300.

People involved in similar meetings elsewhere wanted to be linked; at first there were half a dozen churches but the number grew to fifty. Meanwhile Terry Virgo, Roger Forster, Bryn Jones and several others were emerging as leaders of other networks of new churches. Attitudes began to change. The new church movement became much more acceptable, though there was still some questioning of the apostolic and prophetic aspects. Through its Bible weeks, its speakers at other conferences, its books and especially through its music, it began to have an influence out of proportion to its size. Cobham Christian Fellowship itself began to undergo a series of significant experiences and changes.

In 1990 I was away for the weekend in Leeds and Dale Gentry from the United States was speaking at Cobham. I arrived home to discover that there had been an extraordinary meeting at which he had prophesied that revival would come, that our fellowship would be part of it, that it would touch the royal family and nobility, politicians and entertainers, as well as many ordinary folk. Christ would figure prominently in the media. It would be costly; it would cost us every-thing. At that time there was no sign of revival so this seemed astonishing. He reiterated it the next day and said that God was going to give us our own 'well' to draw from.

It was then that our meetings moved from Cobham to Leatherhead as Pioneer People. We kept before us the vision of the well and of revival. We were reminded too of the personal cost. It was a testing time and from 1991 to 1993 we saw peo-ple leaving the church.

In May 1994 I had lunch with John Mumford from the Vineyard church in south-west London. When I enquired after his wife, Ellie, John told me that she was in Toronto and was experiencing a powerful outpouring of the Holy Spirit at the Airport church there. As he described what was happening I suddenly knew this was what we had been awaiting. That evening we had a meeting at which 400 people were expected. I rang Martin Scott, one of our leaders, and told him what I had heard. We would not mention Toronto at the meet-ing but we would seek the power of the Holy Spirit and see whether what happened was the power of God or auto-suggestion. What we wit-nessed that night was clearly the power of God. The people had no idea what was happening in Toronto but we saw a similar impact. The meetings went on through the rest of 1994 and outgrew the school hall we used, so we hired a marquee for 2,000 people.

In 1995 we took the bold step of closing down

all our activities for a year to concentrate on meeting three nights a week to focus on repentance and prayer for revival. As had happened earlier a good many people drifted away but in 1996 we hired a cinema in Esher for our meetings and once again numbers grew.

In June 1997 the opportunity came to hold Sowing the Seeds of Revival meetings in the large Emmanuel Centre, newly acquired for Christian use, in Marsham Street, close to the Houses of Parliament. Gerald Coates led the first series of meetings involving Roger Forster, Lynn Green and Dr RT Kendall. The meetings, five nights a week, drew over 40,000 people and this total was repeated when Gerald led a second series, four nights a week, in 1998 with musicians Noel Richards, Sue Rinaldi, Caroline Bonnett and Dave Bilborough.

Well over 6,000 people came forward to 'get right with God' and twelve dustbins full of pornography, illegal drugs, weapons, masonic jewellery and personal effects were collected. Members of the House of Lords and House of Commons and staff at Buckingham Palace attended, as well as the homeless off the streets. Over 500 bags of food were distributed to the hungry.

I had not realised how demanding five nights a week of meetings would be. At the time we were also pursuing possibilities for acquiring a large property as the kind of training, prayer and revival centre foreseen in the prophecy. Nothing worked out. Hopes were raised only to be dashed. We seemed to be getting things wrong and I felt a sense of brokenness and humility before there was a breakthrough.

Waverley Abbey House had been run by CWR, for-

merly known as Crusade for World Revival, mainly as a conference and training centre. After speaking at a celebration weekend there on the occasion of Selwyn Hughes' 70th birthday, Gerald learned that CWR was refocusing its ministry and going out to strategic places in different parts of the world. The former stable block, now the east wing, at Waverley Abbey House would be sufficient for CWR's future needs as a base there and the rest would become available. Here was the fulfilment of the vision in the prophecy, not only for Pioneer but for March for Jesus, of which Gerald is a founder. The new ownership is in the name of Kingdom Life Ministries. Gerald Coates is embarking on another pioneering venture with the Lord.

15

Eric Delve

Discovering the grace of God in his service

During a few days away at a conference in Cheshire, I spent the free afternoon with Eric Delve. Throughout his years as an itinerant evangelist he saw the lives of many thousands of young people, particularly university students, touched by God. He then moved to parochial ministry. From this base he continues to exercise a far-reaching influence in spiritual renewal.

He opened up to me frankly about the low points and the failures, as well as the highlights and blessings, of his spiritual pilgrimage and ministry. I asked him first about his childhood in Wimbledon, where he was born to a family from a local Brethren assembly.

I suppose my childhood was fairly strict although I didn't think so at the time, except perhaps when it came to matters like Sundays. My sister Jennifer and I were not allowed to play games and read ordinary things on a Sunday, although my parents became more relaxed as I grew older. I think any child today would find that upbringing very strict, but it was a happy childhood.

I still remember the awful moment when I decided I was going to spend some of my Sunday-school sixpence in the shop on the way. That was sinful in several areas: I was robbing God's work of the money; I was spending money on a Sunday and I was eating an ice-cream, encouraging Sunday trading. I don't think my parents ever found out but I was left feeling very guilty. I was seven or eight and it was a defining moment of my childhood.

For holidays, my father used to fix a sidecar to his push-bike. My sister and I would sit in it and he and Mum would ride to somewhere like the Chilterns where we spent our holiday. My dad nearly collapsed pulling that thing along from Wimbledon with all that weight. Later we got a little car, of which we were very proud as it was one of only three or four in the whole street of about two hundred houses, so we were very much the elite. My father was an instrument maker: one of those rare people who can spot something that is one-thousandth of an inch out in a machining part or something like that. He was a skilled artisan.

At school I was mischievous and failed the 11-plus. My primary school teachers were very angry, saying, 'You should have sailed through that, and because you were fooling about you didn't.' I felt then that I was meant to achieve something. In those days, if you failed your 11-plus you were able to sit it again at twelve. I passed the second time and went off to grammar school: Rutlish, where John Major was, though I don't remember him. Just as for many other working-class boys, it was an introduction to a new world of many possibilities.

Being brought up in the Brethren meant there

was the constant reiteration of what some people call the simple gospel, the good news of God's grace and forgiveness for sinners. At seven years old I did kneel down at my mother's knee and 'give my heart to Jesus' and that was very real to me. I had spontaneously asked her if I could. As I grew up, however, I began questioning. In the Brethren assembly I found the answers were not forthcoming. I was constantly rebuked for using my mind, 'the enemy of faith'.

I found myself floundering, until in my early teens I discovered C S Lewis' books. The first I read was *The Screwtape Letters*. When I read *Mere Christianity* I felt for the first time that it was possible to have a real faith without suspending the mind. It was a liberating experience.

When I was thirteen I joined a Scout group attached to Holy Trinity Church in Wimbledon. I started to go to church parades and I found myself being overwhelmed by the beauty of the language of the Book of Common Prayer. Also, for the first time in my life, someone was making sense of what I could feel during Holy Communion. So the experience I had going to church parade began to mark me.

Eric met Pat in his late teens, during evangelism in the local coffee bar. It was not until later that they got together and were married very young; he was twenty-one and she was seventeen.

Pat had become a Christian through a mission in Wimbledon, but her father was anti-Christian and her mother had been involved in much superstition. As someone from such an unbelieving background, Pat became stressed through the

cultural strictness and expectations of the
Brethren. She could not cope with the closeness of
it; it was too much like being in a goldfish bowl. So
we went to St George's Church in Morden, where
she had been before. We were there for some years
and went through some very difficult times.

We were very young when we married and
were not really ready for it. I allowed myself to get
angry with God because I had grown up with a
very romantic notion that if you were a Christian
everything worked out all right. If you got married
as a Christian then of course your marriage would
go smoothly.

When we hit difficulties and problems I became
very angry indeed. For a couple of days I went
storming up and down the roads raging at God,
pouring out my anger against him. Then I felt
totally exhausted and heard a small voice saying,
'Is that all then?' I said, 'No, there is some more
and you can have the rest of it.' A little while later
the same question came, 'Is that it then?' and I said
'Yes, that is.' Again it was like a very small voice
saying, 'Shall we get on then?' I realised then for
the first time that God really did love me and that
nothing I could do would actually stop that.

I date my relationship with God from that
moment because I don't think that you know
much about the God of grace until you know the
grace of God.

After I left school I worked for an insurance
company. I had a string of clerical jobs; in those
days you could walk out of one job into another. I
spent two years as a fireman and drove a fire
engine round London, which I found enormously

rewarding. I then went into advertising and that was one of my more disastrous times. I got involved in a pretty immoral lifestyle and Pat had another emotional breakdown.

I got in touch with Roger Forster because I had heard that he and his wife were good at helping people with problems. This was the rather condescending way in which I was thinking about Pat. It never occurred to me that I was a main problem. Roger came and talked to her. In the course of our conversation about her I said something rather callous. He said, 'That does it, Eric. I have had enough of you. Don't bother to call because I am not available to you.' He then walked out.

I realised for the first time that Christianity involves the demands of God's kingdom; until then I had thought that it was all one-way traffic. Despite Roger's words I got in touch with him again and said, 'If I am going to change I need to spend a lot of time with you.' He allowed me to travel around with him for about two years, while I was still working in the city. I processed his tapes, sold books and loaded the van. Pat thought I was better off with Roger than swanning around doing who knows what.

That time with Roger was probably as good as going to any Bible college. It was through being with him that I discovered that God wanted me to be an evangelist. It was if God was saying, 'I still want you to serve me in spite of all the messes you have made and all the mistakes that you seem to have accumulated on the way'.

Eric left his job and got together with an evangelistic team for four weeks before the London Festival for

*Jesus in 1972. They worked all over London from the
back of a large truck with a band on board. There were
four big festival meetings in different parts of London.
The final one, in Hyde Park, drew 25,000 people, with
Larry Norman, Cliff Richard, Dana and other celebrities. Someone had the boldness to invite the completely
unknown Eric Delve to speak for four minutes.*

I took seven, to preach. It led to a number of
contacts and was the start of my life as an evangelist for the next 20 years. I joined Youth for Christ
and the family moved to a village in the Midlands,
the base from which I operated as the movement's
national evangelist. I led student missions in
almost every university in the country.

When Clive Calver left Youth for Christ I felt it
was time to move on as well. I founded Down to
Earth with a team of up to a dozen for city-wide
evangelism. By this time we had five children at
various stages of education. Sometimes Pat and
the children would be able to come for a couple of
nights towards the end of a mission, but otherwise
it was impossible.

God appoints seasons and at the end of the
1980s I felt that the season for doing these missions
had come to an end for me. I was accepted for
ordination training and continued as a travelling
evangelist and speaker while attending Trinity
College, Bristol. I found the ordination service in
Bristol Cathedral moving and memorable. I had
this incredible sense of coming home and knowing
this was where I belonged: quite a long way from
the little boy in the Scouts' church parade to a man
in his forties being ordained.

As I looked at the New Testament I saw that

Paul had not spent all of his life travelling. He had gone to some places and stayed, such as Ephesus where he remained for three years. I was asked by the Bishop of Warrington to go to a parish in Kirkdale. We arrived at this little church in inner Liverpool and I stood in the car park outside. It was covered in broken glass, dog mess and food wrappers. Rain was lashing down almost horizontally. I said, 'God, this is a wasteland.' I heard a voice say very quietly, 'Eric, this is a wasteland where people live.' My reply was unprintable but I knew God was saying at that moment, 'Eric, I want you here.'

I had had great ideas about the sort of church that I should go to and they had not included one like this. In fact for me this 'wasteland' became an oasis because I rediscovered the gospel as I saw it applied in the lives of ordinary people, many of whom felt they were unconsidered, disregarded and looked down on. The three and a half years that we had there were amazing. Pat, like me, was not overwhelmed by the beauty of the situation. But the Lord really blessed her and used her there in a powerful way. As far as the children were concerned, our youngest, Grace, our sixth and adopted child, just slotted in straight away. She is a great mimic and adapter, and became more scouse than the scousers. Our son Andrew found life at one of the schools there quite difficult, but he soldiered on and by the time we moved he didn't want to leave.

We then had this call from St Luke's, Maidstone. The way it worked out, we knew it was from God and had no doubts that it was his plan that took us there. We could not have done it if we had not gone first to St Lawrence's in Liverpool. In many ways we compressed experience into that time in Liverpool that would have taken two or three times as long in other places. We didn't realise how much it had cost and how much strain it had been until six months after we left. It took us that long to realise that we weren't on holiday and that houses in this part of Kent do not have barbed wire round every crevice and broken glass on the top of every wall.

At our first Christmas in Maidstone we were able to hold a carol service in the Chequers shopping centre and 2,000 people came. More than half of them were not churched in any way. I found it a powerful indication of how hungry people now are for spiritual reality. The biggest hope for St Luke's is that it will continue to develop as a parish fellowship centre and more so as a regional resource for churches in the surrounding area which may be struggling. We are talking to the New Wine people about the possibility of a New Wine type of event for the south-east, on our county showground at Detling, two miles up the road.

Those are some dreams but I don't want to make the same mistake as before: I don't want to make the work my god, or an idol. I want to stay in touch with the Holy Spirit. My constant aim is, 'Lord, I want to go on being filled with the Holy Spirit and also I want to be clothed with power from on high.'

16

MIKE PILAVACHI

'MY CRAZY IDEA THAT BECAME SOUL SURVIVOR'

When I arrived at the Premier Radio studios, on the seventh floor of Glen House near London's Victoria station, Mike Pilavachi had just finished recording his weekly two-hour Soul Survivor radio show for young people in the London area. He was glad to sit down in a quiet room with a cup of tea and relax, as he told me that it was still early days in this latest venture. The response already was very encouraging. He described it as a learning experience for those involved. Like the whole Soul Survivor operation it is a team effort.

The summer Soul Survivor event in Somerset now attracts over 16,000 young people. There are also festivals in Norway, Holland and South Africa and plans to start in Australia. Mike's is the original vision and the driving force at the heart of Soul Survivor. But he has seen a team grow up together, fully committed to the work and caring deeply for one another.

What of Mike Pilavachi himself? What's his background and how did he come to lead Soul Survivor?

I was born in Paddington, London of Greek Cypriot parents. They had come to England a few years earlier. I was brought up in Harrow and went to school there – not *the* Harrow school but the comprehensive down the road. My parents were Greek Orthodox atheists, so I was brought up in a very non-Christian environment. They had a very low view of the Greek Orthodox Church.

When I was fifteen I wrote a school essay with the title 'Why I am not a Christian'. I chose the title and basically wrote that Christianity was for old people and those who were scared of death, who needed a crutch, who were of low intelligence and who didn't understand that science had the answers.

It must be God's sense of humour that less than a year after I wrote that essay I became a Christian. I had been searching for something and there were some of my friends at school whose wholesome lives attracted me. They told me about Jesus, that he was their Saviour. One February day I read John Stott's little booklet *Becoming a Christian*. I went up on the top of a hill, because I thought I had to do it somewhere special, and I knelt down and prayed the prayer at the end of the book.

I got up not feeling any different but knowing that a change had happened. I had clinched the deal and had passed from death to life. When I became a Christian I said, 'Lord, I want to be a missionary' and I waited and waited for the call. I didn't go into full-time church work until I was twenty-nine. I had to go to university first and then I worked in a secular job.

I started going to church at St Andrew's Chorleywood because I was hurting and broken, not for any other reason. Some things had gone wrong in my life and I knew they prayed for people there. When I had been there for about three years David Pytches, the vicar, offered me the job of church youth worker. I accepted, and that was the beginning.

That was eleven years ago. When the New Wine camps began I took on the youth side. After a couple of years I had a vision of something like New Wine but just for young people. I couldn't get it out of my mind. One day I told David Pytches. He said, 'It sounds like a crazy idea to me, Mike.' But there was a twinkle in his eye and he added, 'But it might just be of God. OK, we'll give it a go.'

In the first year nearly 2,000 young people came to Soul Survivor and the festival has grown by 2,000 each year, to over 16,000. Mike describes the formula.

Basically, we worship the Lord in intimacy, we teach the Word, and we give space to ministry in the Holy Spirit, surrounded by lots of sports activity, bands playing, cafés and other facilities. We are wanting to train young people for ministry as much as anything else and to give them a vision of what they can be for Jesus in the years to come. Worship is at the heart of what we do, but we emphasise that worship is a way of life. Worshipping the Lord in the meetings also means caring for the poor outside and reaching the lost.

J John, Steve Chalke and other evangelists have been regulars at Soul Survivor and we have teamed up with the World-Wide Message Tribe, who do an amazing work in Manchester, reaching out to young people, especially on the council estates and in schools. In the year 2000 we are going to stop the festival for a year and take more than 20,000 young people to Manchester for a week or two of mission, practical as well as evangelistic, linking with the World-Wide Message Tribe and local Christians. We are nervous as well as excited about this prospect.

The team at Soul Survivor has been together a long time. Some of those now working full-time had been in my youth group from the age of twelve or thirteen. Matt Redman is one example; he is now our main worship leader.

Mike Pilavachi and several colleagues felt that if Soul Survivor worked at Shepton Mallett in the summer it would work in their home town of Watford throughout the rest of the year. So eleven of them began a youth congregation. They were passionate to reach the local unchurched young people with the good news of Jesus. The Soul Survivor church now has a congregation of around 200, and 170 in cell groups. Mike takes up the story.

We bought a warehouse in which to meet and we landed in the parish of St Peter's in west Watford. The vicar, Chris Cottey, is now our chaplain. We see ourselves as an Anglican missionary congregation, still linked to St Andrew's, Chorleywood because it 'birthed' us. We have Alpha courses, outreach activities, schools work, cell groups, discipleship training events and the *Soul Survivor* magazine.

We sent eighteen young people out to Guatemala to work with street children with the Toybox charity. If people just sit in the pews at an early age they will go on only being receivers. If we give them space to minister at an early age, even though they may fail, they will grow.

I am single, and what can I say about that? We shall see what happens. I am always so busy and love what I am doing very much. I enjoy being with young people. They are stimulating, they are so open; they are willing to 'go for it', to take risks.

Mike finds it hard to generalise about the new generation but he has discerned a change, a spiritual awakening, among those with whom he is in contact.

I have seen young people recently who have humbled me with their desire to follow the Lord with all they have got. There is one young man who has shown me a song he has written, with the words, 'Lord, have all of me, not just part of me, I want to give you all of me' and he really means it. I know a number of others just like that. It's not hype, it's a serious, thought-through decision to make a commitment to Jesus above all things.

There is a young person in our church, living with his parents, who has started work and has begun giving from his earnings: not a tithe but three-quarters of his wages. Another young man was a student and he worked through the summer doing a vacation job. At the end he gave me a cheque for £300 for the church. He said, 'I did my summer job so that I could give the money to the Lord.'

I could tell you story after story like that. It's awesome, and our responsibility is clearly not to play on that. God have mercy on us – or not have mercy on us – if we manipulate these pure hearts.

All over the country there are young people coming on fire and that is the hope for the future of the church. There are young people who want to lay on the altar their gifts of musicianship, or acting, accountancy, teaching, building, whatever it may be, and say, 'Lord, use me and use my gifts.'

We hear so much in the media about how young people are deserting the church but there is another side to it, there really is.

Let me give another example. At Soul Survivor two or three years ago the stewards discovered on the first night that there was a group of young people who had brought drugs. We decided to leave them for one night – making sure that they did not pass on the drugs to anyone else – and we would see what happened. They came to the meeting that night, and to the meetings the next day, and then in the afternoon they made friends with some Christians at the camp. They all went to a field, sat in a circle and prayed. Those who had the drugs dug up the grass, buried their drugs and then they worshipped. There have probably been cows in Shepton Mallett going cross-eyed but at least the drugs were not in the kids.

When I was a teenager everyone was happy to talk about moral issues, what was right and what was wrong, but no one wanted to know about spiritual things. Now it has gone the other way, and this is our challenge. Everyone is into spirituality but it is much harder to bring in the moral dimension. Christianity is a spiritual faith that leads to a changed morality. There is right and wrong, and as youth leaders we have to grapple with how to communicate that to this new generation.

I have a passion for young people and I wake up in the mornings feeling very grateful that I am working with them, even though I am nearly at my fortieth birthday and may soon be past my sell-by date. Youth leaders have been told that to work with young people you have to be hip, trendy and relevant: green hair, earring through the nose, understand all their music and everything else. I don't know the difference between grunge and garage, jungle and techno – it's all noise to me. I still like Simon and Garfunkel, so I am the last person to be culturally relevant to young people – a big, fat, hairy Greek – but the qualification that Jesus said was needed is to love them.

I have seen some very hip and trendy youth workers for whom it is just a career for a while, and you can feel that there is no love. Some of the best youth workers I have seen have had grey hair but absolutely love the young people. It obviously helps to understand what they are talking about, and to understand their music, but that is not the most important thing.

We are meant to represent Jesus and show love, understanding and trust. That is the Jesus model.

17

COLIN DYE
FROM SWAN LAKE TO KENSINGTON TEMPLE

They suddenly spilt out of the doors of Earls Court, down the steps and onto the busy road. Some fifty Christians, mostly mothers, singing 'The name of the Lord is a strong tower', were going out to invite people to that evening's Mission to London meeting. In the cavernous concrete interior of Earls Court a booming voice was reverberating from the heart of the arena, where some 2,500 people had gathered for an afternoon seminar.

It was there that I was meeting Colin Dye, chairman of Mission to London, to hear the story of his coming to faith and becoming senior pastor of one of Britain's largest congregations, at Kensington Temple. As we walked to a partitioned private section on the next floor I noticed Colin's very upright, lithe frame and his smooth, almost gliding, walk; the movement of someone who had once been a principal in the Royal Ballet. His story begins with his childhood in Kenya and Australia.

My father's side goes right back to the early settlers in Africa. A man called Gouch Dye went over on a clipper sailing ship from Norfolk. My mother settled in Africa with her parents because her grandparents were stationed in East Africa during the war and remained there afterwards. There was no missionary connection. My father's side were adventurers and it was private enterprise which drew my mother's family there.

My father was involved with farming machinery and everything connected with it. He also opened petrol stations. We travelled quite a lot around Kenya and also Tanzania – Tanganyika as it was then.

I have two brothers, one older, one younger. When I was seven the family sailed from Dar Es Salaam for Australia. The situation in East Africa had become unsettled after independence. There was not going to be much of a future for the white settlers.

It was a happy childhood, with lots of outdoor life in Africa and Australia. We headed for South Australia, for Kalgoorlie, an outback former gold-mining town; very rough and ready, a bit like the old Wild West in films. There was still some gold in the old slagheaps. When the rain came we children found specks of gold there. One child even found a nugget.

By this time I was showing my artistic side, which eventually found expression in dance; very unlikely, quite out of the ordinary, in that kind of environment. My parents gave tentative support. I had not seen ballet before but there was a teacher of tap dancing, highland dancing and ballet. I went to each of these classes and took to ballet like a duck to water.

The family then moved on business to Western Australia, to Perth, where I was able to go to ballet

school. This led to my performing on television
with the Western Australia junior ballet company.
My talent was spotted by a formidable lady
named Madame Kira Bousloff, from the famous
Ballet Russe of Monte Carlo. She trained me in the
Russian style.

By the age of sixteen I was ready to go to
England and the Royal Ballet School. I sent photos
and informed them I was coming. I was told that I
could not be accepted without an audition. I managed to persuade my parents to let me go and I
went over alone. On arrival at the Royal Ballet
School I was told that I shouldn't have done this
but reluctantly was given an audition. I was then
accepted on the spot.

*Colin's parents had split up, his father went to
South Africa and died there. A couple in Carlisle, members of the Christian Brethren, became Colin's legal
guardians in England. Colin's older brother Raymond
visited Britain, about a year after their father's death, to
see how Colin was getting on. Raymond had found
Christ and told Colin of his experience. Colin's
guardians invited Colin and his brother to spend
Christmas 1971 with them. They all went to a meeting
together in a nearby village, to hear Dr Alan Redpath.
He preached on 'Wilt thou be made whole?' and said
that the only one who could make that possible was
Jesus. He asked 'Do you want to be like Jesus?'*

Everything within me said 'Yes'. That week I
knew God was calling me into full-time Christian
service. In a very strong prophetic revelation I saw
the need – and felt a strong call – to work among
drug addicts. I was ready to leave the Royal Ballet
School but my guardians felt that it was right

before God to finish my training and then fulfil
what I was trained to do.

I was glad that I did. I now have three years of
professional dancing behind me. I travelled widely, was doing principal parts, was in the corps de
ballet and was partnering the senior ballerina. At
the end of the three years, however, I knew that I
had to leave. The time was then right.

I found a Bible college in Cambridge at which
to study and it was in the Brethren assembly in
Cambridge that I met Amanda, who became my
wife. I was a fully-fledged Pentecostal but went to
the Brethren assembly there because it was so
evangelistic. Amanda was nursing in Cambridge;
she was a senior sister for many years. We have
two children: Elizabeth, sixteen, and Laura, thirteen.

I then worked for two years at a Christian reha-
bilitation centre for drug addicts. So the call that I
experienced when I committed my life to the Lord
was fulfilled.

*The centre was associated with Kensington Temple
and it was there that Colin worshipped in London and
was baptised by Eldin Corsie. After his work with the
drug addicts Colin was sent for four years for an
'apprenticeship' in ministry at an Elim church in
Bournemouth.*

*He was then called back to Kensington Temple by
Wynne Lewis, who had become senior pastor, to be his
associate. When Wynne Lewis became the Elim general
superintendent in 1991, Colin Dye was named as the
new senior pastor of Kensington Temple . . .*

It came upon me suddenly. I realised that I was
sitting on the other side of the desk and wondered

how all this had happened. I had started as a church worker, deacon, elder; I came right through the ranks. But that was instructive because I realised that ministry is about service.

The following year was the first Mission to London with Morris Cerullo at Earls Court, a stone's throw away from Kensington Temple. He had had meetings at the Royal Albert Hall and many people from our church had attended.

We felt as a church that we should be involved, but in the first year or so I was a little cautious because few people outside Morris Cerullo's circle seemed to appreciate his ministry. So for the first year I was just helping on the sidelines. But the more I got to know him the more I realised his love for the lost and his desire to equip the body of Christ. I was able to see beyond the Americanisms and realised that here was a major ministry which was of value to London.

After several years Morris began to speak about handing over the mission. The time came, and it was totally his initiative, for him to move on. He handed over Mission to London to my chairmanship and a group of executive leaders from different churches; 1998 was the first year without Morris Cerullo at all and we felt that it was a transition which went well.

The vision for Mission to London is for it to be a combine harvester, one of many. I compare the Alpha course with Mission to London. We know that the Alpha course does not touch the type of people who come to the mission, and vice versa. I ask people to understand that events like Mission to London have a part to play and are just as valid as every other means of evangelism and training.

I believe that the Holy Spirit is giving a strong prophetic word to the church at present concerning holiness and harvest. Some years ago, when I was a young pastor, I had a sermon title, 'Why be holy when it is so hard?' I was to preach on the motivation for holiness. I was having lunch with some ministers and we started talking about sermon titles and whether we needed them. Someone said that my sermon title was a bad one because it mentioned holiness. Everyone laughed. But he was serious; he said, 'Never put something like that in your sermon title because people don't want to hear about it.'

When I went home I felt burdened that people didn't want to know about holiness. I began to pray and felt the Holy Spirit say to me – just an impression – that the time would come when people would flock to any service or conference simply because the topic was holiness. There would be a hunger for holiness in the people of God and it would precede a harvest.

I have held on to that over the years and now I am seeing it start to happen. It is my biggest encouragement. I believe that the real work of repentance and purging and holiness is coming. It will be the final preparation for genuine harvest.

POSTSCRIPT

Those who have featured in this book may appear to be 'special people', yet every person in the body of Christ is special. Ordinary people can be used in extraordinary ways. At his ascension the risen Christ was prepared to leave a small band of ordinary people to continue his mission on earth. This motley group had already proved to be weak and unreliable and slow to learn. They had even deserted him before the crucifixion. Yet these were the people chosen by Christ to start his church and to carry on his work.

Their temptation would have been to start straight away, with their own plans and ideas and their own enthusiasm. If they had done so the whole enterprise would soon have failed. It was not their mission, it was the Lord's, and they did not have to 'go it alone'. They were to be empowered by the Holy Spirit. They, and the women, had to return to the city, to the upper room, where they had to wait, to pray and to be prepared. Then, on the day of Pentecost, the Holy Spirit came upon them with transforming power.

They became the first 'passionate people' for Christ. There has been 'a passionate people' in each generation since. It is amazing that the Lord chooses to take *us*, the kind of people we are, and change us by his Spirit as we open up our lives to him. He then wants to use us in his church with the gifts he has given us, and to use us as his agents where he has placed us in the world, as part of his purpose. We are rediscovering that the church is people of all kinds, worshipping together, learning together, strengthening one another, sharing one another's burdens and going out into the world as Christ's servants.

Some Christians always seem restless, wondering whether they are in the right place. When our lives are fully committed to the Lord, we *are* in the place of his choosing, unless he clearly shows us otherwise. When we are willing to do anything and go anywhere for the Lord we may be led to uproot, take an entirely unexpected course, go to a different place and enter another culture. Or we may know that we should stay put, just where we are, because that is where he wants us to serve him. That may be just as challenging. We are called to be 'salt' and 'light' wherever we are. There are those in 'secular' jobs who may be the only Christian where they work. Their presence represents a little bit of God's kingdom in that place. God has a plan and purpose for the life of each believer and it is through prayer that we become attuned to his will.

At every stage of life we need to be open and willing to stay or to move, as the Lord would direct. I have known people in their seventies who have embarked on relief work overseas. Even those who are infirm and housebound can have a ministry of prayer, and how vital that is.

There may be situations in which the Lord's word to us is 'Wait', as it was to the disciples before Pentecost. Times of waiting can be very testing but are part of our discipleship.

Finally, a prayer. I don't know the source of it, but I first heard it many years ago. I have treasured it and now use it sometimes before the blessing when I am leading a service.

Lord Jesus, Master Carpenter of Nazareth, who on the cross through wood and nails wrought our full salvation, wield well your tools in this your workshop; that we, who come to you rough hewn, may be fashioned to a truer beauty and greater usefulness in your service; for the honour of your holy name. Amen.

JOHN WIMBER
His Influence and Legacy

Edited by David Pytches

John Wimber was a spiritual giant – both physically and spiritually: a vivid example of how God raises up and uses the most unlikely people to build his church. How this former rock musician, heavy drinker, atheist and some-time drug user gave his life to Christ and became, in many people's views, one of the most influential church leaders of the twentieth century, is related in this moving tribute by the people who knew him best – his family, his friends, his colleagues and fellow Christians.

Edited by David Pytches, this book contains reflections on John's ministry as a musician, theologian, church planter, businessman, leader, writer, encourager, friend, husband and founder of the Vineyard Church.

Contributors include Matt Redman, Graham Cray, Gerald Coates, Terry Virgo, Jim Packer, Sandy Millar and Carol Wimber

0 86347 277 X

COMPASSIONATE CARING

Trevor Hudson

Exploring Prayer Series

Whilst travelling one day from the black African township of Soweto, to his affluent white parish on the outskirts of Johannesburg, Trevor Hudson received a vision. *'The simple words that typed themselves across the screen of my mind was to take members of my congregation to where your brothers and sisters are suffering.'*

The story of the subsequent 'Pilgrimages of Pain' undertaken by the church are recorded in this moving book. But the message is much more than simply an account of bridge-building. The author stresses that our spirituality is worthless if we do not use it to engage ourselves in a broken world and come alongside our suffering neighbours. If we profess to be followers of Christ our prayer, worship and fellowship must overflow into expressed care for those in need.

'Our times cry out for a gospel-shaped spirituality that is both intensely personal and deeply aware of our suffering neighbour'.

0 86347 295 8